"So long, Fare
Auf Wiedersehen
& Goodbye"

Lee Hammond

"Until we meet again".

Table of Contents.

FOREWARD.

ollowing on from my first publication "Never the Cold War Hero" which was
n insight into the first half of my career this covers the final 10 years of my 22
ear engagement.

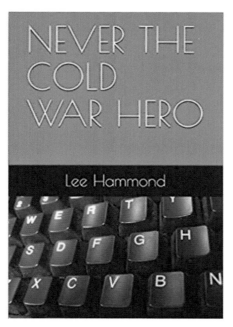

1y story gives a personal insight of time serving Her Majesty Queen Elizabeth
. After most of my career was spent during what was commonly referred to as
The Cold War". The final 5 years witnessed the effect on the Armed Forces of
1e United Kingdom following the collapse of the Berlin wall in 1989.

here have been and always be a vast choice of publications from former
ervicemen/women recalling heroic and exotic adventures. This, however, is a
ory of a normal enlisted airman and his wife who upon discharge from the
iilitary became just Mr & Mrs.

1 my 22 years I was never sent to any exotic locations. I was never decorated
or any campaign and I never even managed to walk away with the notorious
Long Service & Good Conduct" medal.

Vhen I finally left the Armed Forces on 31st October 1994 it was to be a
ownward spiral for too many years. For some the adjustment to civilian life
an is an experience that can lead to serious mental & health problems. Some

find it impossible to adjust, adapt or even accept the civilian way. I was one whose whole life would collapse. It took me many years to recover any sort of normality in life but those years taught me a lot about myself along the way. Some 27 years since handing in my identity card (RAF Form 1250) I am still struggling with the loss of a lifestyle.

Towards the end of my career I started to become bitter and twisted. This was because the longer I served the more I noticed the continual decline in numbers and resources of Armed Forces defending our Nation. Personnel levels and equipment were cut by successive governments that in my opinion had no understanding or caring for the defence or security of the United Kingdom.

This publication is dedicated to all those who served in the communications roles of Royal Air Force Trade Group Eleven. It was an honour and pleasure to serve alongside you.

Special thanks also for two of my "Lyneham Lovelies". Annie Roberts & Andrea Roberts (not related) have been of great assistance throughout the writing of this book.

Annie & Andrea. My little helpers.

Copyright Lee Hammond 2021

All rights

Chapter 1.

Royal Air Force High Wycombe.

August 1984 – December 1986.

(Officer Territory).

Returning to the United Kingdom was a time of opposite emotions for Elaine and myself. She was happy to be home after a somewhat torrid time in Germany. I was very downbeat about the whole thing. Being posted to the stamping grounds of so many "senior officers" would not have been in my top 100 of posting preferences. This station was yet another non-flying base and housed the Headquarters Strike Command along with the United Kingdom Regional Operations Centre.

We had a few weeks off before I had to show my face at work, so it was decided to spend some family time together. Mother-in-law was taken in tow and a tour of the Trossachs was arranged with national coaches. Seven days on a coach trip may just bring us all together a little bit more. For me it was a week of total boredom, old people, ancient coach which kept breaking down and swarms of midges. After the delights of German beer at more than acceptable prices the return to paying for British booze was a shock to the accounts department. Would not have been so bad if the quality were anywhere near the German standards, (Bavarian purity law of 1516AD). Everything worked out in the end as Mother-in-law enjoyed the trip and Elaine was speaking to me again.

We got settled into a nice little airman's married quarter (155 Kilnwood), this was located next to the High Wycombe base and made walking to work no more than a 10-minute journey across the road. I was on a high at this time in my career because after my annual assessments from my time with 11 Signals Unit I had the ambition to enter the Sergeant's Mess within the next 3 years.

At work due to the fact it was the largest Headquarters for the RAF I found a large group of comrades who were mostly to become good friends. The section consisted of a main communications centre, a separate section for all the NATO landline links and an exceedingly small radio room. The radio room was the least used area and mainly used for flight watch duties. In fact, it was normally so quiet in there that you could complete a whole 12-hour shift without getting a single call from any aircraft. When one did come in there was a massive scramble by all the radio trained personnel to be the first to get to it and respond.

It was a great atmosphere with on the whole friendly and very efficient people on the shift. There are far too many names to go through now so I will list them at the end of this chapter. The one I will however mention now was Brian Proctor. Brian was "the Boss". Warrant Officer Brian Proctor proved to be one of the most tolerant and understanding people I ever worked for.

In 155 Kilnwood the boxes were slowly unpacked and everything put in the correct place. The atmosphere was somewhat cool as Elaine and I were slowly drifting apart. We had only been in the house for a few weeks when suddenly there was a new addition to the family.

Sunday lunchtime and we were walking up the road to the Cpl's club for the usual pre-lunch drinks. I stopped in my tracks as I could hear a little "squeaking" in the grass. Seeing a few blades of grass move I approached expecting to see a mouse scarper off before I got near it. Nothing of the sort, there was a tiny little tabby cat lying in the grass and not looking in particularly good condition. This kitten was obviously a member of the semi-feral cat families that lived in the heating pipe tunnelling by the Sergeant's Mess. I picked it up and was instantly attacked by an army of fleas and other bugs. As I cradled it in my hand it just closed its eyes and rolled into a tiny ball of fluff.

Now, contrary to popular belief, I am a soft-hearted so-and-so. I could not leave this tiny kitten to the elements or worse. We went straight home, put down some whisked egg and water on the kitchen floor and left the poor little mite. The session that followed in the club was the shortest ever in my social history. 2 pints went straight down without touching the sides. I do not think Elaine even finished her half pint of lager. Straight back to the house to check on the little fur ball.

Bless him, in the short time we were away he had done his business from both ends and left us little welcome home packages. That night I never went to bed. Just sat in the chair with this defenceless creature on a cushion on my lap. Next morning it was straight down to the Vet in High Wycombe. This gentleman was obviously not the most caring of souls, "I will put it down for you now" he said. "Not a chance" was my reply. "It has ticks, fleas and a heart problem, so it is kinder" he stated. According to this lover of all creatures great and small, Sammy (yes, I had already named him), was not weaned and would not last more than a couple of days. Treatment for the fleas and other wildlife was urchased and off we went back home. Sammy was to become our best friend or the next 20 years. He was a cat but he thought he was human and wailed like baby instead of meowing. He enjoyed all the luxuries of life, was partial to ny cheese, unsalted butter, chocolate, chicken curry, kebab and so on.

Our best friend ever. Sammy (1984-2004).

o ingratiate myself with those responsible for writing my annual assessments, I ined the committee for the RAF High Wycombe Corporals Club. For some ason I got the job of Secretary. This role was known as a "secondary duty". Iaving these duties usually got you a few more smarty points from those who eld your career in their hands.

Jaine in the meantime had wasted no time in finding employment in High Wycombe town. She now had full independence and I saw little of her during ie week. As we were back in the U.K. the luxury of military transport into ocal towns and amenities was no longer available. Purchase of transport was eeded. I found myself a Honda CX500 plus mother-in-law paid for a Talbot Iorizon hatchback. So fully mobile we could now explore the local region. My notorcycle was given a name, as all my 2 wheel beasts were since getting my riving licence years earlier. This one was christened "Tinkerbell". The car emained nameless as I have always been a biker at heart and a motorcar was to ie just "mode of transport". Motorcycles have souls and you tend to get ttached more to them than a tin box.

The best cared for CX500 in history.

We were now in the latter half of 1984 and the annual assessments were due for all of us. Being called into the office for mine, given by Brian Proctor, I would have been very content with a standard "above average" rating. To my total surprise, as most of the previous years had been spent with Rod MacLennan and the crew in Germany, my efforts there were taken into consideration for this annual "palm sweating" event. When my numbers were explained my jaw just dropped. 8,8,7 with highly recommended for promotion. It was a great day at work and an excuse for a party session in the NAAFI that night with the lads of the shift. My time at Headquarters Strike Command had got off to a brilliant start. My best mates on the crew were a couple of senior aircraftmen, Chris Thornton and Nick Martin were a real pair of comedians who like myself enjoyed a drink or two. That evening in the NAAFI bar was one to remember.

Home life to my surprise had not really improved at all and we both went our separate ways. I think if it had not been for us both having so much affection for our little bundle of fluff, Sam the cat, one of us would have had the courage to leave and find some alternative accommodation. It was rapidly becoming a marriage in name only. Elaine was now spending more and more time with her civilian workmates and friends. Sometimes, she would go out after work on a Friday and not be seen again until sometime the next day. Voices were never raised but it was evident that we had by now totally drifted apart.

I put all my effort into what was left of my career and concentrated on the two important parts of keeping me in with a chance of promotion: work & secondary duties. Work was not much of a problem as even though I say so myself, I was a good tradesman and a more than competent junior manager. On the secondary duties front I ended up as the Secretary of the newly formed Corporal's Club, it was me or nobody else because nobody else wanted to do it. This wonderful social centre was the most popular social facility on the whole complex. I think this would be because when the NAAFI, Sergeant's & Officer's Mess called "last orders" we remained open to supply those with the need of further alcoholic beverages. The bar was also manned by members of the committee and it could be a nice little boost for the monthly income for the member doing his/her bar duties for a week. I will return to the stories from the club later. For now it is back to the work environment.

Every few months, it was, as on most military establishments, exercise time. These could last any time between 24 hours and 3 days. When they did it meant everybody was put on a 2 shift system so the normal days off were ignored and everybody went to work. It was basically, in for 12 hours then home for 12 hours. Because it was an exercise all the usual bars were closed for the duration. There was a civilian public house in the local village (Walters Ash) but the risk of being caught in there was not worth it.

For those of us who were lucky enough to work for Brian Proctor, any exercise was an easy change to the normal routine. When an exercise was called half of his crew would accompany him to the "fall back" communication centre at RAF Bawdsey, Suffolk. Luckily, Mr Proctor always picked the usual members of his crew to travel with him and set the whole system up. Thankfully, I was one of the chosen few. Into a 3 ton Bedford truck we would bundle with enough clothing, shampoo and shaving cream to keep us smelling reasonable for the duration of our absence. We would turn up at this isolated dump early in the afternoon. After proving identity to the obligatory RAF policeman on a picket post, we would disappear into an underground complex, never to be seen or heard off until the end of the exercise. Everything we needed was there and our role was purely to maintain communications with the outside world if something nasty had landed on High Wycombe and caused a catastrophe. This never happened so we were never really needed at any time (thankfully). As soon as all was back too normal we would load up the truck and head for home to hear stories of commissioned officers running around like "headless chickens" while wearing respirators and tin hats. This was in all my service career the only place I ever saw officers wearing their rank insignia on a Nuclear, Biological & Chemical protective suit.

The Corporals Club was my main escape route from the problems with home life. I threw myself fully into the role of Secretary and along with some of the other committee members made the whole thing a total success. Being involved with the running of the club gave all of us a chance to be "responsible" for the bar. This was taken in turn and each member had a week at a time in the role of barman. I hooked up with Clint & Elaine Tookey. Elaine was a chef in the Sergeants or Officers Mess so her skills were very handy. This is how the system worked: On a Monday all the bar stock was signed over to the lucky individual(s) who would carry out the role of "Mein Host" for that week. The following Monday you would then sign over the stock to the new committee member taking over. The only money that was handed over was the cost price of the stock you had sold. This meant any profits were kept by the outgoing barman. It was a great system, the more you sold meant some worthwhile pocket money. Because Elaine Tookey was supplying her cooking skills we were able to offer a range of solids to the customers. Baked potatoes, chilli-con-carne, chicken curry and sandwiches were all available. All the profits from this money spinner were split 3 ways. The Tookey/Hammond partnership proved very profitable for the rest of my time at High Wycombe. Due to the popularity of our establishment we had more than our fair share of SNCOs & Officers being invited in by various Corporals from around the camp. Back in the 1980's there were still restricted pub opening hours. This meant that at 2300hrs we would call last orders and lock the front door. All who wished to continue drinking were more than welcome so long as the customary tip was added to the cost of each purchase, another little income booster for us behind the bar.

Due to a total lack of interest from some of the committee members, our turn for bar duty seemed to come around monthly. I was grateful that about half of the committee had only volunteered for a role to gain "smarty points" on their annual assessment. It just meant more pocket money for us three. I must at this point thank my boss, Brian Proctor and his middle management team. They had no problem giving me all the time off from shift work to carry out my secondary duty. Also, had full support from my work colleagues.

I did put on my uniform and go to work sometimes though. One day-shift will remain with me for the rest of my life. I was summoned to Mr Proctor's office and requested to go to the police control point to escort a civilian from the Ministry of Defence to the Commcen. As I ambled towards the entry point I noticed our dutiful RAF policeman checking this person's identity and issuing his visitors pass. I could not believe my luck. Our visitor was none other than the nemesis from my instructing days at Cosford, GRUNDY! I took one look at him and asked for his identity card. Knowing he had just shown this to our control point policeman it was just to annoy him a little. I studied the document in detail just to keep him waiting and noticed it stated his rank as Sqn Ldr

Retired). So in my eyes he was no longer serving and was a civilian. I handed it back to him with a jaunty "thank you". His response was, "I did not hear Sir from you Corporal". I stared back and responded with, "I call serving officers Sir" because I have to, I call civilians "Sir" only if I respect them, follow me please". It was a case of Hammond – 1, Grundy – 0. I had that warm sort of smug and satisfied feeling for the rest of the day. I was not requested to escort him out after his visit was over.

The year of 1985 was rolling along nicely both at work and socially. By this time, our marriage was a farce. Elaine led her own life with her own friends from High Wycombe. I meanwhile concentrated on having a fantastic time with not only my work colleagues but with my good friends in the Corporal's Club. Not every minute was spent in the bar as our extremely poor darts team entered one of the local leagues. Somebody also got together a 10-pin bowling team to take on the American teams at their little base in High Wycombe. This meant a few trips away to basically have as much fun as possible. On the bowling nights we usually turned up a bit worse for wear and continued the drinking session while attempting to hurl a 16lb down the correct lane. Our American cousins took the whole matter very seriously. They all wore team shirts, had little gloves on the left hand (if they were right-handed). I still do not understand the point of the glove, but it must have been worn for a reason. Somehow, we always managed to put on a good performance. At the end of the first season we even managed to win several trophies, much to the disgust of those who took the whole thing in a serious manner.

Now the darts team. Well that was a totally different thing. To put it bluntly we were all useless. At times it was difficult to even see the board, let alone hit the thing. For some unknown reason we very rarely lost the final round of the evening (the beer leg). After an entertaining evening in the world of Civilians our minibus would collect the usual rabble and head straight for Desborough Road in High Wycombe. On this street was possibly one of the best Chinese take-away establishments anywhere in the United Kingdom. If I were out for the evening doing my "Eric Bristow" impersonation, Elaine would wait up for me. Not to make my homelife difficult but she would tolerate seeing me for her portion of Chicken Curry. Sam the cat also got his portion which he lapped up lovingly. Another favourite of his was Doner Kebab. Once the chilli sauce took effect his little paw would frantically wipe his mouth like a windscreen wiper on maximum speed. Every single darts team in the league would cherish the visits to our home venue, the Cpl's Club. Thanks to Elaine Tookey they were treated to a fantastic selection of cold buffet trays. Also, when in their own pubs they had to call "last orders" at 11pm. None of that rubbish with us. It could be well past 1am before any of them fell out of the door onto their minibus with a very impatient driver on-board.

On a rare occasion Elaine and I would be seen out together. We were particularly good at giving the impression that all was well in the Hammond household. My attitude was that what happened in the 4 walls of 155 Kilnwood, stayed within those 4 walls. However, for me things were about to take a massive downward turn. Elaine always got the bus to and from High Wycombe which was fine for me. On one occasion she asked if I could collect her as the local bus operator was going on strike that day. No problem I said. I knew where she worked as previously I had picked her up on the motorbike. Off she went as usual and I now had the pleasure of just sitting around for the day until picking her up at about 3pm. It was a pleasant enough day, so I fired up the Honda and took it for a spin around the leafy lanes of Buckinghamshire. Great fun doing "the ton" on country lanes. As I had not been out in the car for a lesson in a while, I thought I would give it a run up to London and back on the M40. Well I got to London, turned around to come back again but never made it. I was travelling behind a low-loader truck carrying scaffolding. Doing the correct thing I indicated my intentions to overtake. Next thing I knew was a scaffolding pole hitting the side of my head. This nasty piece of metal had come straight through the windscreen and proceeded out of the back window. The car then proceeded to bounce off the central reservation barriers and side swipe the lorry I was trying to overtake. In the meantime, the rest of the scaffolding poles and planks were making a hasty exit from the back of his truck. Some rattled across the 2 lanes of the motorway and the rest managed to dismantle my car in no time at all. All of this took place in but a few seconds but for me time really did slow down. When it was all over, there was the truck pointing up the bank at the roadside. What was left of my Talbot Horizon was sat in the outside lane of a motorway. A chunk of the engine had replaced the passenger seat and only 1 door was still attached. I casually crawled out of the car and closed my driver's door behind me, sat on the crash barrier and lit a smoke. A daft thing to do at the time as there was oil and petrol leaking everywhere. First on the scene was a RAF Regiment friend of mine. Tom could not believe his eyes when he saw the state of the car. He and a colleague were returning from a Ground Defence Training day at one of the London bases. Expecting to find body parts all over the place he just stood and said, "Is that you, Lee". I could just make him out through the blood dribbling down from my forehead. All praise to the Buckinghamshire Police Force, they got to the incident within a couple of minutes of it happening, swiftly followed by the ambulance crew. In the rear of he ambulance I was patched up and they were surprised to find that nothing was broken or missing from my body. The genuinely nice young Police Officer explained that I would have to blow into his machine to ensure I was in a fit condition to drive at the time of the incident. He did however offer to wait until I had been taken to hospital and given treatment. "Let's get it out of the way now", was my response. I puffed hard into the little tube. What seemed like a lifetime passed and then he explained that unfortunately I was just in the "not fit to drive" category. That meant I would be taken back to the Police station in High Wycombe and processed for action against me. He was nice about it and almost apologetic because it was only just in the red. I never had experienced a police cell before, and I never want to do it again. After being processed and formally charged my friendly Police Constable took me home. "Let me go in first", he said. He looked at Elaine and said, "Don't shout at him, he has had a shit day". I thanked him, looked at Elaine and went upstairs for a bath. She did ask me how I was and showed genuine concern. I must be honest and state that at that time I did not care what my wife said or thought as the love once I had was fast ebbing away. Now I had to face the music from "Top Boss", Brian Proctor, and all of those above him.

My court summons arrived, and I was appointed a Commissioned Officer to attend with me and represent Her Majesty's Royal Air Force on my behalf. For the first time in years my "best blue" No 1 uniform was taken out of the wardrobe and dusted down. Off we went to the Beaconsfield Magistrates Court and waited to be called in. Surprisingly, the owner of the other vehicle was in the same waiting room. He was being prosecuted for having an unsafe load and causing the incident. To be honest that did not make me feel any better, but it was to have some input to the outcome of my punishment. My Flt Lt advisor just gave me one piece of advice, "best behaviour Corporal". "No problem, Sir". We were called in and a list of charges were presented to me. Naturally, I pleaded guilty as charged. All but 4 of the offences were dropped. This left only 4 offences for me to be punished for. Prior to the final sentencing I was asked, "Do you have anything to say"? I offered my humble apologies and then my Flt Lt gave a glowing report on my service to date. He stated that my actions on the day were "totally out of character". Now this was another commissioned officer that I had total respect for. The outcome was a fine of £200 and a driving ban for drink/driving and not having a qualified driver with me of 1 year. As we left the court my new hero Flt Lt said, "You have a gifted life, you were damned lucky there". Maybe, just maybe it was all behind me now and I could get back to some sort of normality. The next 2 days saw the usual military banter comments from all who knew me. Nobody could believe how lucky I had been.

Come Friday morning that was all to change. The weekly edition of the Beaconsfield Echo was published, and I was all over the front page. "Airman comes down to Earth with a bump" was the page 1 headline. The gutter press had one of their "hacks" at the court and they made a meal of my misfortune. Needless to say, because of this the Royal Air Force were going to take an even dimmer view of my behaviour. A couple of days later I was up in front of the Station Commander on a formal charge. Everybody thought my military career was going to come to a sudden stop. I thought the same as I had not exactly been the perfect JNCO over the last couple of months. I was charged with bringing the Royal Air Force into disrepute, something that is about as serious as you can get when serving Her Majesty. Do not ask me why but when I walked into the office to face the music, I felt I would end up doing a spell in a Regional Detention Centre swiftly followed by a visit to the Job Centre.

However, the outcome was an official "Formal Warning". This meant that if I stepped out of line in any way over the next 12 months it would mean a dishonourable discharge. Walking out of the office I must have sighed one of the biggest sighs of relief in history. Now I really did have to behave and just put this whole episode behind me.

Next time I went into work I was immediately summoned to the office of Brian Proctor. Because of my recent behaviour, my security clearance had been removed (again). This meant that I was not cleared to work in the Communication Centre or any other sensitive section. However, Brian managed to get me transferred over to the Telephone Exchange. This section was as usual run by the lovely ladies of "the lumpy brigade". They knew what they were doing so I let them get on with it. I just spent my time in the office checking the landline records and bill payments to British Telecom. It was not a real job, but I was safe for now. I did at least have the common sense to realise that any progression in rank during the next 9 years of my career was to say the least very slim.

My next challenge was just to keep a low profile and avoid any situation that could end up with me in front of the Station Commander. I had just got comfortable in the telephone exchange when I was requested (not ordered) to see Mr Proctor in the Commcen. In I went with a somewhat bashful approach. What had I done now, that I did not know about? In his office I was informed that a posting had come in for me. My next tour of duty would be with No 1 Maritime Headquarters Unit in London. This was a Royal Auxiliary Air Force unit. My only dealings with these people prior to this had been when they would visit our Communications Centre for training at weekends. Was I impressed with them? Not really. More on that to come later in my next chapter.

When I went home that evening and told Elaine I was posted, I really hoped she would say that she would not be going with me. Sadly (at that time), she said she would be moving to London with me. I could have said "Not a chance" but maybe there was still a small spark of love and affection inside me towards her. Getting everything moved to the new home at Hendon was going to prove a problem as I had no driving licence. Once again, my friends and former shift-workers came calling when needed. A bunch of the lads helped load the van for 2 trips up the M40 and beyond. I cannot remember who was behind the wheel, but his driving standards were much appreciated when shifting the 4-foot fish tank. Christ Thornton got the short straw and ended up sitting in the back of the van on both trips. First trip he had to contend with a half full fish tank slopping water all over him. Second trip he spent the whole journey grimly hanging on to a Honda CX500 motorcycle. Thanks Chris you were and are one of the best. I did not have the heart to tell them beforehand that our Married Quarter was up 6 flights of stairs in a block of maisonettes at Royal Air Force Hendon. Getting the washing machine up that lot was a nightmare. Move completed I bid farewell to some of the best people I worked with and for. In 1984 when I was told I was posted to Headquarters Strike Command I was not impressed. When I left in 1986, I left with a heavy heart because most of these people had become not simply good friends but possibly some of the best friends. As this chapter in my life ended, I wondered "Why is Elaine still here?".

With thanks to Brian Proctor, Chris Thornton, Neil Verdon, Leroy Blake, John Gibbs, Paul Johnson, Al Mack, Ian McDonald, Frank Gilroy, Nick Martin, Les Binns, Debbie Marshall, Ivy Lay, Bev Childs, Sandy Mountain, Keith Bromage, Colin & Lin Jones, Diane Harrington, Mick English, John Cousins, George Anthony, Robert Lloyd and even Brian McInnes. Finally, all those that I have failed to mention due to ageing of the grey cells.

Chapter 2.

1 Maritime Headquarters Unit, London.

December 1985 – July 1987.

(Civilians pretending to serve).

Before I go in-depth with this chapter, I must give a short explanation of, The Royal Auxiliary Air Force unit that I was about to be involved with.

The Royal Auxiliary Air Force (RAuxAF) was formerly known as the Auxiliary Air Force (AAF). During times of conflict in the past the members of this force were a vital part to the defence of the Country. To be honest, without them the Battle of Britain in 1940 may have had a different outcome? In November 1959 Parliament announced that 3 Maritime headquarter units would be formed and manned by personnel of the RAuxAF. These were to provide backing in the Operations Rooms and Communications Centres that were controlled by Royal Air Force Coastal Command and the Royal Navy.

The new units would be based at Northwood (1MHU), Edinburgh (2MHU) and Plymouth (3MHU). Volunteers, men & women between the age of 17.5 and 45 need not have had any previous service experience. Full training existed in whatever trade they wished to work. This training was undertaken by qualified members of the Royal Air Force. All 3 of these units would need training in the maritime roles available at the time and communications currently in use.

My new place of employment would be Valency House, Northwood. This building was about half a mile from the Joint Services Headquarters, Northwood. Because this was primarily a naval establishment, it was called: HMS Warrior. Why the Navy would call a base on the edge of London a ship still baffles me even today. So back to Valency House. Formerly, the Chateau de Madrid Hotel it stood in a couple of acres of prime London real estate. The whole site is now occupied by luxury (unaffordable) housing.

My only encounters with any of these part-timers was somewhat limited. While at High Wycombe we would have them working alongside us and learning from the expertise of regular forces. They usually turned up a couple of times a year and it was always the same few faces. They seemed keen and willing to learn so had no reason to think badly of them. This opinion was soon to be abruptly altered.

We had been allocated a married quarter some 10 miles across London at Royal Air Force Hendon. Formerly our residence had been an Officers married quarter. This meant that the standard of basic furnishing was of a somewhat higher quality than is usually on offer to enlisted servicemen. The carpets in all rooms were wall-to-wall. Oh, how the other half live. It was a nice maisonette and we even had a garage attached to keep my Honda 500 safe and secure. It was still some 11 months before I would be allowed back on the road. Having the garage gave me peace of mind that "she" would be safe. This was important as the married quarters were adjacent to what must have been one of the most undesirable council estates anywhere in the United Kingdom. It was a complex of multi-storey flats surrounding a shopping centre. The sight of a security guard in the paper shop was novel to me at the time. The one and only pub got one visit from us and that turned out to be enough. Stained furniture and sticky carpet along with some less than desirable customers soon convinced us not to make it our local. The biggest eye-opener of the whole thing was the milkman. He would drive around and stop outside each dwelling, load his goods into a little bottle carrier. Then he would cover the whole wagon with security shutters to ensure nobody could help themselves to the goods. Having never lived in a metropolis like London before this whole experience was totally new to both of us.

I turned up at Valency House after we had got settled in and was amazed by the somewhat laid-back approach by the 7 other regular staff. There was a Flight Lieutenant (Adjutant), his role was to look after the day to day running of things and sort out any mess caused by the commissioned side of the part-timers. His staff consisted of 1 sergeant, 1 senior aircraftman and 1 leading aircraftman. The latter was straight out of trade training, so he was getting an easy posting at the start of his career. I have tried but just cannot remember the names of these gentlemen, except one. Kevin Pratt was the Senior Aircraftman. For obvious reasons it is not hard to remember his name. Anyway, I rolled up on the unit and introduced myself. The adjutant took me to his office and did the usual welcome. "Have you arrived anywhere?" he asked. "Not yet, Sir" was my response. He called in the Sergeant clerk and told him to send one of the lads round HMS Warrior with my arrival card, getting the required signatures to show I was now officially here. From that first meeting with my new boss I had both a liking and respect for him.

Valency House. Home of No 1 Maritime Headquarters Unit.

As this was formally a hotel the building had a lot of spare space. Upon entry of the main door there was a massive stairway in the middle of the hall. Either side of the stairway had 2 massive reception rooms. The one on the left was now the "Officers Mess", on the right was the "Other Ranks Mess". Down past this was a fully equipped kitchen. Each had their own bar as well. Going up the stairway, the admin offices were in front of you. The training staff office was off to the right. Entering this office for the first time I was given a warm welcome by 2 Senior NCO's. Flight Sergeant Fred Vann was the same trade as me. For the first time in my career I had met a Flight Sergeant that I would work well with. The other character was Roger Scutt. His trade was Air Electronics Operator. Being a Master Air Electronics Operator meant he had reached the pinnacle of his trade. MAEOp is the maritime aircrew rank to our Warrant Officer. Not trying to be funny but Roger could go no higher without, selling out and taking a commission.

It got to the point where I just had to ask: "What is the training programme?" I thought they were going to cry with laughter. Fred tried to keep a straight face and said that I would be responsible for training the communications element of the unit. This would be easy as all were only trained as Teleprinter Operators. There was no training for them in the fields of Radio Telephony or Wireless Telegraphy. Roger then threw a spanner in the works by saying "If any of them turn up". This led to an in-depth conversation which gave me a clear picture about the whole unit.

There were the 7 regulars who kept things running. On the Auxiliary side there were some 70 part-timers (civilians in uniform). Each year they had to attend a certain minimum of training hours. While doing this they were given full rates of pay (variable according to rank), generous travel payments (a lot better than urs) and finally a £600 bonus at the end of each financial year. Basically, it was a good little earner. With about 25 of these people being "commissioned officers" it was a very lucrative organisation to be involved with. The rest were split down the middle. Some were involved in the Air Electronics element; all the others were mine for the taking. So, in theory I was responsible for about 25 communications operators. It was up to me to keep them up to speed on the current equipment's and procedures.

Now the hours were by no way strenuous. All I had to be there for was: Each Monday & Thursday between 7-9pm and one weekend each month. The rest of the week was my own time. This whole thing was turning out to be a real eye-opener. I had heard of "cushy" postings in the Royal Air Force, but this was unbelievable. The Adjutant popped his head into the office and told me to take the rest of the week off. The next weekend was a training weekend so if I returned on the Saturday I would be introduced to the unit. This would give me a clearer picture of who I was dealing with. So, it was paid time off in the new home with Elaine getting everything sorted and letting Sam get used to his new surroundings. Elaine immediately set to work on sourcing her own income. She came up trumps at the first attempt. Her new place of employment would be the Government Public Health Laboratories in Colindale. Just a short walk from home. The job was a lab assistant dealing with germs & diseases from around the world. She was to prove good at this because later during our stay they would offer to pay for her to get a degree in some sort of medicine and then progress in her role. She had to sadly refuse this offer, due to us leading a transient lifestyle. Neither of us knew how long she would be in her current position. Thankfully, all the weird and wonderful germs she was working with were left in the laboratories.

Everything was running like smoothly and at this point all was happy in the Hammond house. Maybe, just maybe our marriage problems of Germany and High Wycombe were all behind us. My current role was giving us a lot more time together and we were making the most of it. Still serving my driving ban due to stupidity some 3 months earlier we were totally dependent on public transport. The nearest underground station (Hendon) was less than a 10 minute walk away. With an endless stream of buses from every direction meant no problems in getting anywhere. It is true what we say in the North of England. The "Southern Softies" are spoilt. Over the years I have noticed that public transport further north than the Watford Gap is totally underfunded by central government in London. I suppose if everything is perfect for them why should they care about the common masses that voted them into positions of power.

Anyway, enough politics, for now. It was time to go and do some work. Luckily, the Royal Air Force supplied a transport service for those who lived at Hendon but worked in Northwood. This saved me having to travel via the underground into the centre of London and then back out again to Bushy, the nearest tube station to Valency House. Throwing my uniform on for the first time in almost a month I made sure I was smart enough not to give any officer a reason to have a moan at me. Even my hair was within regulation length, for a change. Because of the timing of the service mini-bus I was back at work with plenty of time to spare. Roger and Fred were not far behind me and we just sat in our office waiting for everybody else to turn up. For some reason, all the regulars arrived well before official "kick-off" time. This was normal for regular service personnel, no matter which service uniform you were wearing. The Auxiliary Air Force obviously had not been informed of this tradition as they were turning up in dribs & drabs. It was almost 10am before the last of my lot rolled in. Strange how all of them seem to have logged in at 8am. Who am I to question this, after all I am the new kid on the block. For some strange reason they all headed straight to their respective messes, apart from the senior officers who headed to the office of the unit Wing Commander (another civilian). Fred took me down to the "other ranks" mess and introduced me to all of those who were carrying ranks of sergeant and below. I took the communications lot to one side and said: "Right, what time do we start training?" The response was a bit of a shock. "Oh, we have not got time for training, we have to get the mess ready for the function tonight". Walking out of there I asked Fred "what are we doing here". His reply was straight forward enough, "we have to be seen". The rest of my day was spent either in the office with Roger and Fred or in my empty classroom checking through the training aids which just happened to be about 10 years out of date. Not once was I summoned to the Wing Commanders office for a "welcome to my unit" speech. Chatting to Roger I just happened to mention that the adjutant never once mentioned my formal warning from my previous unit. Apparently, he was not bothered about my past, only my present. Once again, I had fallen on my feet. There was nothing I could do wrong in this sleepy hollow that would blot my career in any way. The unit had their social functions in the respective messes on the Saturday evening and when I returned on the Sunday morning, not one of them was in a fit state to do any training. Basically, the weekend of training had been a total wash-out. I was learning fast a lot about the Royal Auxiliary Air Force of 1985. Throughout my time here I was expected to attend some of the "social functions". This was not a problem as Valency House had plenty of room for me to arrange a sleeping area. Washroom facilities were excellent as well. The only thing missing was a full breakfast delivered to my room.

The next day was a normal Monday except it was also a "training" evening. Because I had to be there for the 2-hour training session at 7pm I decided it was not viable to go home for an hour just to return. Into Bushy to buy a donar kebab for tea. Roger who was renting "digs" in Watford always stayed behind and had a selection of delights in the kitchen cupboards. Apart from beds, Valency House had all the comforts of home. Chilling out at these times Roger would give me his military history. He had been in for about 5 years longer than me and his whole career had revolved around the Avro Shackleton & BAE Nimrod aircraft. It was blatantly obvious where his heart was. If he was in the air, then he was happy. Some of his stories about low-flying over the North Sea & Atlantic looking for illegal fishing boats or Soviet submarines had me glued to every word. It is a crying shame that he never lived long enough to get all his adventures into print. To my total surprise I had somebody to teach that evening. 3 members of the communications staff were in the classroom awaiting a couple of hours of outstanding instruction from yours truly. Strangely, these 3 faces were familiar to me. It was the same ones who turned up at High Wycombe to put the training into practice. During my short time with No 1 MHU they would become friends. The approach from these individuals proved to me that some of the part-timers were serious about the role they had taken on. As for the SNCO's and Officers, let me put it bluntly, they did "bugger all".

At least I felt I was doing something worthwhile because 3 people really did want to improve their skills. They even asked if I would teach them the basics of Morse code. Why not! I loved anything to do with radio communications. We soon got into the system of Monday was refresher training for communications working. Thursday was basic training in deciphering the dots and dahs of morse code.. I just accepted that on every training weekend there would be no training because they had social functions to arrange. I was getting the hang of this part-time environment quite quickly.

The Easter break had arrived and that meant a total shutdown of the whole unit. Elaine was working as normal, so I spent an inordinate amount of time cleaning and polishing the motorcycle stored away in the garage. The few days she did get off work were spent chilling out with the occasional visit into the city of London. This period of rest & relaxation was soon over, and it was back to work for both of us.

Just as everything was settling down nicely, Fred was posted. This was good for him as he had been wanting to move for a while. We all assumed he would be getting promoted to Warrant Officer, he had more than earnt a progression to the top of the tree in ranks for the non-commissioned officers. No such luck, the excuse from the promotion board which had sat earlier in the year was: "out of mainstream communications for too long". I mean, that is so stupid. A man with his experience and skills had been passed over because he had been instructing part-timers. He was gutted and I can understand why. It occurred to me that if he had been passed over for promotion then what about my chances of ever getting in the Sergeant's Mess? Alarm bells started ringing in my head and I now had decided to get away from here as quickly as possible.

Farewell Fred, it was an honour and a pleasure to have served with you.

Maeop Roger Scutt, Cpl Lee Hammond and LAC? with 7 auxiliaries who took their role seriously at RAF St Mawgan, Cornwall in 1986. Flight familiarisation with the BAE Nimrod.

By the time his replacement joined us in the office I had established myself well within No 1 Maritime Headquarters Unit. I even got a "Good Morning" of their Officer Commanding. It was only a short while until I found out why he had noticed me. The Monday after he had spoken to me, he showed up at work. For several weeks after that he would turn up every weekday, sit in his office and look busy. The poor man had recently joined the ranks of the unemployed. He was job searching from the unit rather than sitting at home doing it. I am sure this would have been a great relief to his wife. At least he was not under her feet all the time. With him being in all the time it meant that the office staff had to behave themselves as their office was next door to his. For us instructors, it made no difference whatsoever, we were hidden out of sight in our little "den".

 I know I was not impressed with the organisation, but I did strike up friendships with a few of them. A few of the commissioned officer brigade seemed reasonable as well. The officers who attempted to take the role seriously would at times consult me over any military or moral problems they were encountering.

The replacement for Fred was as different as "salt is to pepper". Les Mann had arrived on the unit. I had known Les from my days as an instructor at Cosford. He was a Sergeant then and I must admit I never got to him when he was a fellow instructor. Elaine had been one of his students in her trade training days back in 1975. He was responsible for her leaving Cosford with the required typing skills, even though she could only, and still can only type with 2 fingers. Alright, I know I fiddled a few final board results to get trainees through the final hurdle only because I knew it was due to exam nerves, each one of these trainees went on to be a benefit to the trade of telecommunications. But Les Mann allowing anyone using 2 fingers typing a pass was pushing it a bit far. 2 fingers will never get you to the speed of 25wpm! He arrived with a promotion to Flight Sergeant and I accorded the due respect he was entitled to. He had grand ideas of re-vamping the training programme, so I left him to it. In my heart I knew he was wasting his time. He was new and would learn the same way I did that most of the part-timers regarded the whole set-up as a social club.

It only took a few weeks for Les to concede defeat. He then hid away in the office working on his favourite hobby, building dolls houses. No, you did not misread that. He built massive dolls houses as a pastime. That was not my only concern as he drove a Lada Riva car. I mean if that is not the sign of impending crackdown, I do not know what is! Springtime came and went leading to a seasonable summertime. Les seemed to both Roger and I to be acting more and more strangely as time went on. We just thought he was getting a little eccentric in his older age.

Life at this point was running smoothly. Happy at work and incredibly happy at home. Elaine brought this to an abrupt end when she announced, "I am going to High Wycombe for the weekend". I had honestly believed all that was behind us but obviously it was not. Off she went on the Friday and as it was a "training weekend" I had to go into work but was back on the Saturday night to look after my best friend. Elaine was back home on the Sunday when I got back from work and the atmosphere was back to 9 months earlier. Thankfully, she was going to work each day, so we did not have to share our home that much. Suddenly she said that her friend from High Wycombe was coming to spend the weekend with us. I never liked this "lad" last time I met him, and this dislike was now getting to hatred level. He turned up on the Friday and Elaine was a little too friendly for my liking. He left early that weekend and then a blazing row ensued. I had made the decision, enough is enough. Packing my bag and moving out was extremely easy for me. I could just move into single accommodation at HMS Warrior. I explained to Elaine that she would have 6 weeks to find alternative accommodation before the RAF took the married quarter back.

Turning up at work with a couple of suitcases did not go unnoticed by the adjutant. He asked if he could assist in any way. Within minutes he had sorted out a room for me and wished me luck in sorting things out. It was a 4-man room, not perfect but somewhere to rest my head each night. Trying to adjust to being on a "ship" was entertaining. The junior ranks mess was called *"the galley"*. The accommodation block was called *"the mess"*. The ablutions room was called *"the head"* and if you walked on the grass, somebody would shout: *"Man Overboard"*. Strange lot these navy chaps who we referred to as *"fish-heads"*. The Royal Marines we called *"Grunts"*. As the adjutant had given me as much time off as I wanted, I started the hunt for a little flat. Watford was not too far away and a lot cheaper than Northwood/Bushy, so the search was on. As I was living the life of a single man, I was invited to spend the Saturday with one of the Auxiliary girls. She was a nice girl but a lot younger than me. At 19 she was almost young enough to be my daughter. Anyway, I accepted the invitation. Her parents had gone away for the weekend so after flat hunting in the morning I turned up at the address given. I was warmly welcomed and then had to endure several hours of listening to songs by an American artist who goes by the name of "Meatloaf". It was a relief to get out and finally down a few beers in the NAAFI to end my day out. I rolled into work occasionally and on one visit the adjutant called me in for my annual assessment. I did not expect much as I had a couple of weeks of my formal warning to finish. 7-7-7 was way above my expectations. At least this kept me in the hunt for a promotion, even if I was not in "mainstream communications". The end of my first 2 weeks as a single man approached and to my surprise Elaine phoned me at work (lucky to catch me there). She was going to High Wycombe on the Friday and asked if I would look after Sammy. Daft question because she knew I would jump at the chance of seeing him again. It would be nice to sleep in my own bedroom again after the pleasures of shared accommodation.

Friday came and sadly it was not the end of my working week. I had a "training weekend" to look forward to. At least my 3 reliable auxiliaries would be there to progress with the Morse code training. They were doing well by this time and had reached about 6 words per minute (WPM). I caught the shift transport over to the married patch and went in the front door expecting a nice quiet evening with a few beers and the company of my loyal mate, Sam. I had only been home bout 15 minutes when Elaine walked in. I have no clear memory of what ranspired over the next couple of hours but somehow, we were back to being a normal married couple.

t was from that point that everything seemed to go faultlessly. In the space of a ew weeks I had served my year under formal warning, which was all behind me now. At the same time, I was able to get my driving licence back and have he freedom of the open roads again. All I had to do now was keep my nose lean and avoid upsetting anybody in authority, then maybe I might get a romotion in the next 5 years.

es finally lost the plot and decided to do it with style. It was a Saturday vening on a training weekend. Naturally, there were social functions in both ness bars. Along with Roger I was in attendance, we decided to try a little xperiment as it was the end of the financial year. The auxiliaries had just been aid their "annual bounty" money for attending the minimum number of hours ver the past year. We stood beside the bar and I announced: "Now that you ave your extra cash, is anybody going to give these two instructors 10% for eaching you everything you should know"? There was a deadly silence from he masses. They were all having a jolly time when I was asked to go out into he entrance hall. Stood at the top of the stairs was my Flight Sergeant, in his niform. Why he was wearing his uniform left me bemused to say the least. He lowly came down the stairs, threw open the door to the Officer's Mess, strolled p to the Auxiliary Wing Commander and promptly started prodding him in the hest. He then proceeded to explain to the poor man, how he should be running is f****** unit. There was a deadly hush for a few seconds. Les was then scorted out of the building by the Adjutant to his beloved Lada car. Off he rove. Both Roger and I found this whole farcical event extremely entertaining. he next day was officially a training day so I was somewhat surprised when es never showed up for work. Maybe he was having a day off the recover his omposure!

Monday morning came round and even before I got near a cup of coffee I was ummoned to the adjutant's office. He looked at me stone faced and said "Cpl, ou are now totally responsible for telecommunications training on the unit". Before I could get the word "Why" out he continued, "Flight Sergeant Mann vill not be returning to the unit". It transpired that the Wing |Commander was a ittle put out by the actions of Les on the Saturday evening. Oh well, it was just ne and Roger left now. We proved to be a good team, and everything ran moothly. I was really getting settled into this "easy" life when suddenly news ame through that the 2 communications roles on the unit were being scrapped.

Instead of having a Corporal and a Flight Sergeant there would now just be a Sergeant to oversee the training for communications to the auxiliaries. This was the start of cost cutting days by the Ministry of Defence.

It was currently the annual assessments were due and I really was not expecting a decent group of numbers or a glowing write-up. I was still under scrutiny for a while due to stupidity at High Wycombe. The adjutant called me into his office and went through the routine. My write-up was glowing praise and he had decided that 7,8,8 would be a fair assessment. I was speechless but very appreciative of his report. With what had happened to Fred I was still determined to get posted and with the cut in establishment it would not be long.

I was fully aware that my days here were numbered and it would soon be back to Elaine having to pack up the house ready for yet another move. Then out of the blue a spanner was thrown into the works. Royal Air Force station Hendon was being closed. Because of this everybody was given a couple of weeks to move across London to RAF Uxbridge. I did request an extension on the deadline, but "jobsworth" took over. Boxes packed and Ministry of Defence foots the bill for the move. We got a nice little house on the main base area. Just a few minutes' walk to the shops and everything else you need. Elaine could continue working at the Public Health Laboratory because the trip to work on the underground was easy for her. We decided to just unpack the essentials as both of knew our stay would be a noticeably short one. Three weeks later my posting came through so once again the Ministry of Defence were going to have to pay for another move.

I arrived on this unit with an open mind about the Royal Auxiliary Air Force. I was leaving with the following opinion: During the 2nd World War and for a period after that, they were an important and much needed element of defence for the United Kingdom. However, in the 1980s they were just another of the endless ways the defence budget was being wasted on non-essential personnel & equipment. Out of the whole group I would miss only a few of them, total number being less than the fingers on my hands. Please do not take this as my view of the whole organisation, I am fully aware that even today some of them in various other trades are invaluable to the Royal Air Force. The medical branch carries out wonderful work. Other squadrons also appear to take the whole thing much more seriously than the Maritime Headquarters Units.

As I stated earlier in this chapter, Valency House was sold off and is now private housing. Due to its location you can buy a rather nice property for around about £2.4 million. If this is out of your price range, go for a small studio style flat for a mere £300,000+. Sadly though, the old house came to an incredibly sad end. In the late evening of 11th September 2020, the building was alight, some say accidental, but others claim it was deliberately set a-blaze. The historic building was severely damaged.

Roger and the most of the regular staff had been great to work with and I would miss them for a short while, especially Roger for his humour and patient approach to every situation. I had no idea at that time that I would never see Roger again.

On 30th April 1990 Avro Shackleton (WR965) took off from Lossiemouth, Scotland at 8:00am. The aircraft was operated by No 8 Squadron and using the callsign *Gambia Zero 8*. It travelled 150 miles to the Outer Hebrides. It was taking part in a military exercise (Ex Bushfire) when it was involved in an accident. The radar onboard had been turned off due to the parameters of part of the exercise, which involved "mutual training" with a Tornado 3 aircraft. Early reports by eyewitnesses led to accusations that a missile strike was responsible for bringing the aircraft down, something that the RAF denied.

Just before 12:00 the pilot radioed ahead to RAF Benbecula to ask for an approach, stating that the aircraft was 20 miles out. Permission was given for a landing from the west. The aircraft was seen to circle at least twice by RAF personnel on the island prior to it crashing into Maodal, an 800ft (240m) high peak near the village of Northton.

The weather at the time was described as "poor" and WR965 was said to have been flying at a low altitude.

A normal operational sortie for a Shackleton in the AEW role, consisted of a crew of ten; a pilot, a co-pilot, a flight engineer and seven other personnel operating the equipment on board (three navigators, a fighter controller, two air electronics operators and a corporal technician).

One of the crew was Wing Commander Stephen Roncoroni, who was the officer commanding No. 8 Squadron at the time. Also, among the crew was Master Air Electronics Operator Roger Scutt (aged 40 years). Roger left his wife and teenage daughter well before his time.

Rest in Peace my good friend Roger (1950 – 1990). We had some great laughs.

Next stop for us was going to be Royal Air Force station Fylingdales. Located on the bleak North Yorkshire Moors.

Chapter 3.

Royal Air Force Fylingdales.

July 1987 – September 1989.

(Ballistic Missile Early Warning Site III).

Back on the road again. Our last 2 moves had been easy to accomplish as the trip from High Wycombe to Hendon was only 25 miles. Nipping across to Uxbridge from Hendon was a mere 15 miles. Getting to Fylingdales was going to be a major operation. Somehow, I had to get the motorcycle, Elaine and Sam all the way up North. It would mean 2 trips at least. Thankfully with it being the height of summer the journey up on the trusty Honda would be a good one. Arrangements were made with the station family's officer at Fylingdales for me to get some keys to a house. The married quarters for all ranks were some 12 miles away from the base in the picturesque town of Whitby. We were offered 3 Derwent Road and it was a nice 2 bed semi-detached. I even managed to get a garage just across the road for storage.

Castle Park estate is situated on the west-cliff side of the town. There is a good pub/hotel just a short walk from the "quarters patch". Across the road is Whitby golf course, more on that later.

Taking the keys was the first hurdle out of the way. I had covered over 250 miles to get there so I needed an overnight stay before heading South for the family. As we did not have a car at the time, and I was still only on provisional licence for 4-wheels it was a case of using public transport to get all up North. Firstly, we had to use the underground to get from Uxbridge to Kings Cross station. Sam was placed in his basket and we both hoped he would not get too stressed by the whole thing. Next it was east coast train up to Malton. This was the nearest station to our destination, some 30 miles away from Whitby. After my comments earlier about the amount of London buses available I stand by my comments about "Southern Softies". The only bus available from Malton to Whitby was a 90-minute drive over the North Yorkshire Moors. To make things more difficult the service consisted of 4 buses per day. Thankfully, RAF Fylingdales arranged to have us picked up at the station and driven directly to our new home.

The North Yorkshire Moors are a bleak and barren land with a scattering of villages and not much more. However, there was one site that not only being a

"Top Secret" military establishment was also a big tourist attraction and on the A169 from Pickering to Whitby. Outside the track to the base was bunch of "ban the bomb" types. These grubby individuals were camped there for periods of up to a week. After that they would all disappear for a few days, hopefully to have a wash. They could only take life camping on the moors for a few days at a time. You could see Royal Air Force Fylingdales proudly perched on the top of the moorland. I had read that when it was being built the locals were in uproar. It was given operational status at the start of 1964. Apparently it made the region a prime target for attack by the "other side". When the "golf balls" were going to be dismantled and replaced by a single pyramid in the late 1980's they were up in arms again because they had come to love the site. Nothing stranger than civilians!

The "golf balls" of RAF Fylingdales, on a rare sunny day.

Sam was as good as gold the whole trip. He slept through the most of it waking on occasion for a drink of water. At the end of an exceedingly long day Elaine seemed happy with her new home and Sam was exploring a reasonable sized garden, digging little holes to do what was needed after holding it in all day.

All we needed now was for the removal team to turn up with our belongings.

Expecting the delivery to be made tomorrow we were pleasantly surprised when a large Britannia Removals pan-tech lorry drew up outside. They had a good journey up so decided that they would do the drop and head back South a day early if we were in. Now we were not going to say "go away until tomorrow" were we. During our first evening at home we got a call from the next-door neighbour. He was Harry McMenemy. Harry was Sergeant in charge of the Communication Centre at Fylingdales and would be my immediate boss.

He and his good lady, Alberta were to become close friends over the next couple of years. I already had somebody to show me around a totally new area.

After a few days of getting settled in we had to get back to normal. Elaine set about finding employment. North Yorkshire has one main industry, tourism. She had decided that would be the best option. Applied for a job as a "chambermaid" with the Royal Hotel Whitby and got in straight away. It was perfect for her as she will freely admit to not being a "people person". I mean, how many people staying in a hotel notice the house-keeping staff, not many. I dusted off the uniform and wandered up the road with Harry to catch the transport to Fylingdales. This somewhat dated coach was an old Wallace Arnold holiday coach. Along with 1 other out of Whitby, 2 out of nearby Scarborough and 1 out of Pickering it was the shift transport to get to our place of work without being noticed by any unfriendly eyes. To this end, even though we were in uniform we had to wear civilian jackets. Apparently, this made us look like tourists doing the sites of the region. We knew we were safe because nobody would notice half a dozen Wallace Arnold buses turning into a military base several times a day, 365 day of the year, would they?

The A169 sign pointing where to have a protest.

Before I describe my time there, I must give a little bit of background of RAF Fylingdales and why it is here in the first place. Fylingdales is a Royal Air Force station on Snod Hill in the North York Moors, England. The motto of the station is "Vigilamus" (Latin for: We are watching"). It is a radar installation and part of the Ballistic Missile Early Warning System (BMEWS). As a part of intelligence-sharing arrangements between the United Kingdom and United

States of America, data collected at RAF Fylingdales is shared between the two countries. The primary role is to give both governments warning of any ballistic missile attack. This is part of what was commonly known as the "4-minute warning", during the Cold War period. A secondary role is the detection and tracking of orbiting objects: Fylingdales is an integral part of the United States Space Surveillance Network. As well as its early-warning and space-tracking roles, Fylingdales has a third function – the Satellite Warning Service for the United Kingdom. It keeps track of spy satellites used by other countries, so that any sensitive activities within the UK can be carried out when these satellites are not overhead. The armed forces, defence manufacturers and research organisations use the facility to their advantage.

While the station is a British asset, operated and commanded by the Royal Air Force, it also forms one of 3 stations in the United States BMEWS network. The cost of this network is funded by the United States of America. The other 2 stations in the network are Thule Air Base, Greenland and Clear Air Force Base, Alaska. All data obtained by Fylingdales is shared in full with the United States where it feeds into the US-Canadian North American Aerospace Defence Command at Peterson Air Force Base, Colorado Springs. For this reason, there has always been a USAF liaison officer stationed alongside the RAF personnel.

Even before commencing operations in the early 1960's, RAF Fylingdales has been subject to criticism from various groups such as the Campaign for Nuclear Disarmament (CND). However, the Ministry of Defence (MoD) defends the use of the facility, regarding Fylingdales as part of the UK's contribution to counter any military threat. They state: "although ballistic missile attack is a minor threat currently, this could change in the long-term, if yet unknown enemies develop missiles as a means to overcome large distances to strike at the UK.

I tend to agree with the MoD statement as to the reason for Fylingdales existing. As for the CND and the rest of the protest groups, no comment!

The journey to base on a somewhat tired coach was about 12 miles and took the best part of 30 minutes. This was due to the age of the transport and having to struggle up the 1:5 incline of "Blue Bank" to get up onto the North York Moors. At times it was such a struggle the bus would come to a complete halt causing mayhem behind it. Harry was with me so got me onto the base with a temporary pass until I could get arrived and issued with everything I would need for instant access. We drove through what in those days was a reasonable amount of security. Approaching the operations site, I wondered when we get off this bus. It pulled up at the massive complex and a door opened for access. In it drove down a tunnel and stopped at a disembarkation point right in the middle. The alls were given site numbers. No 1 was a massive radar dish. No 2 was the operations room and communication centre along with a few offices. No 3 was another radar dish. It never looked this big from the road, but I was really impressed with such technology from well before the start of my military career. Harry then escorted me to the small office next to the communications centre. As I entered, I was greeted by the smiling face of the one and only Warrant Officer Rod Mclennan, He was the Station Signals Officer for Fylingdales. My boss from happy years at Hehn was now my boss again. This was the perfect start to my time in the wilds of North Yorkshire. From the little office that housed Rod & Harry I was taken next door to the Communications Centre. Another familiar face was on shift at the time. Dave Stewart was at Hehn when I was misbehaving all the time. He was accompanied by a solo aircraftman. This made up the manning for the section. There was a technician handy if we mere operating staff broke any of the equipment. I did recognise some of the equipment as it was the standard used throughout RAF communications. The rest however was totally alien to me. One end of the section was full of American equipment supplied for our links to the USA. It was explained that about 80% of all the signals traffic we handled was directly to our cousins across the pond. I would need to be trained by the USAF in the correct use of their equipment. It transpired that our technicians were the lucky ones with this training programme. They were packed off for a couple of weeks to America for the instruction. We humble operators had the pleasure of visiting RAF Croughton, Northamptonshire for a couple of days. A trip to Croughton was sorted out for me and in no time I would be competent enough to use the awfully expensive looking systems. As it was summertime the ride down to Northamptonshire was enjoyable.

Although it was called Royal Air Force Croughton, the base had been a United States Air Force establishment since 1950. Home to the 2130th Communications Group it was a new experience to me. The only other time I had ever been on a military establishment of the United States was to visit the shopping facilities at Wiesbaden, central Germany. I arrived at the main gate to be greeted by a massive hulk in combat clothing. He was carrying enough firepower to deter any attempt at illegal entry. When I explained why I was there he asked me very politely to report and sign in at the guardroom. As I walked across he bid me Welcome to Croughton air base, Sir". As I signed in another large gentleman carrying the same number of armaments shuffled a few papers and said Welcome, Sir, we hope you enjoy your visit". By this time I was getting confused. My identity card showed my rank as corporal but everybody was calling me "Sir". This was getting a bit unsettling. Maybe they did not know what a corporal was! When I finished filling in forms for a pass and permission to leave the trusty Honda on base, I asked for directions to my accommodation. He looked at me and requested I take a seat in the office and help myself to coffee. Being a lot bigger and stronger than myself I complied willingly. 15 minutes or so passed and in walked another hulk in combats. He took my bags and bid me to follow him. Naturally I complied with the order. Outside the building was a minibus and in we jumped. He drove no more than 200 yards and stopped outside what looked something like the Officers Mess. He picked up my bags and asked me to follow him. Going through the front door I was convinced a mistake had been made, this was the Officers Mess. Behind the reception desk was a very smart civilian with full collar & tie. He asked to see my identity card which I handed over without question. At this point I knew they would find that a mistake had been made. Really I was supposed to be in a tatty wooden hut with 39 other bodies to remind me of my days at Cosford. How wrong I was. He asked me to sign a register and handed me both my ID card and a single key. "Follow me please, Sir". By now I am in a state of total confusion. Down a corridor we went. "This is your accommodation, Sir. If there is anything you require the reception is manned 24 hours". Off he went and left me to get on with it. I opened the door and was totally "gob-smacked", the room was massive. It housed a 4-poster double bed, the largest television screen I had ever seen with everything available from across the pond. Now back in 1987 the United Kingdom had 4 terrestrial television channels and that was it. On this cinema screen sized thing there were hundreds to choose from. The furniture was of quality manufacture unlike the cheap rubbish most of the single serving personnel accommodation on offer from our government. In the corner of this large room was a fridge stocked with various drinks all costing $1 per bottle. There was also an ample supply of chocolate bars and snack packets all at a mere 50 cents. This little palace would be my home for just 2 nights but it was like being in a top class hotel.

My evening meal in the "Mess hall" was another cultural eye-opener. The selections were never ending. I was tempted by the T-bone steak, which was the size of a dinner plate. On this was placed a mountain of mixed salad and something like 1kg of "French fries", the Americans do not call them chips. My choice from the sweet trolley was a knickerbocker glory which stood about 30cm high. Wonderful food and the over-the-top polite staff made the whole thing a pure pleasure. Next stop would be a refreshing shower in my palatial bathroom before sampling the evening entertainment venues.

Everything you could ever want was within the confines of the perimeter fencing so there was no need to wander into the local village for a beer. First top was the "Enlisted Club". There was a massive choice of drinks including a few decent quality English beers. Only had a couple as I would need a clear head for the training tomorrow. Then on to the bowling alley and enjoyed "chucking" one down the lanes, it brought back memories of Germany and High Wycombe only this time I was sober.

The training which was just me being shown everything by an expert lasted a day and a half, then it was time to head back to Yorkshire. This was my first experience of life with the Armed Forces of our allies and I left being amazed at how well they are looked after. Nothing was left to chance when it came to catering for their every need. The only thing I missed was a real English breakfast. I am not a fan of flap-jacks with syrup so early in the morning.

Once back at work I was teamed up with Nick Matley as my partner on shift. Nick was single so he lived on base, for me it was the Wallace Arnold luxury coach to work alongside the "Scopies". They had a much larger manning for each shift, (1 junior officer, 1 flight sergeant & 5 sergeants). During the good weather I would always get the motorcycle from the garage and hit the "ton-up club" along the A169.

It was at this point in my career (15 years) that I should have received my long service and good conduct medal. Due to my moment of total stupidity at High Wycombe it was explained that the award at this time was impossible. The issue of this award would be reviewed in 5 years' time. Fair enough I thought because I had done the long service bit but had to confess my conduct was not something to be proud of.

My trusty Honda 500 was showing her age now and it was decided a replacement should be purchased. I could not resist parting with £600 for a slightly larger model. This was to be my last motorcycle as I was getting to that point in life when riding in wind and rain was no longer a pleasure. It was another Honda and had a little more power than the 500cc twin. It was the CB900F, had 4 cylinders and a top speed more than 120mph. Whitby to Scarborough on the coast road was great fun when the sun was shining.

Honda CB900F outside our married quarter.

Elaine was well settled in her new employment and I had now got my feet under the table at work. Both of us happy in this wonderful town of Whitby. After the dirt and noise of London this was like stepping back in time. The people were friendly and always willing to have a chat, unlike the lifestyle before our move. Remember, if you ever catch a tube train in London, do not try and strike up a conversation with anybody. If you do all you will get is a cold glare from everybody. Although only a small town Whitby is home to so much for visitors. It has a long maritime history which was associated with exploration and unfortunately whaling. One famous name is the Royal Navy Captain James Cook.

James Cook (1728 - 1779) was born not far away in Great Ayton. When he was 16 he moved to the fishing village of Staithes to be apprenticed as a shop boy. It is believed that this was where Cook first felt the lure of the sea while gazing out of the shop window. After 18 months, not proving suited for shop work, Cook travelled to the port town of Whitby to be introduced to John and Henry Walker. The Walkers were prominent local ship-owners involved in the coal trade. Their house is now the Captain Cook Memorial Museum. Cook was taken on as a merchant navy apprentice in the Walkers fleet of vessels. These ships were used to ply coal along the English coast.

He eventually joined the Royal Navy and the rest is, as they say, history. A replica of his most famous ship HMS Endeavour can still be seen in Whitby harbour today.

HM Bark Endeavour entering the harbour.

Another famous connection with the town is the author Bram Stoker. His gothic horror novel "Dracula" (first published 1897). In the story Count Dracula is washed up on the shores of Whitby while travelling to England from his castle in Transylvania. It was Stoker's visit to the town in 1890 that provided him with atomspheric settings for his novel.

The history behind Captain James Cook and Bram Stoker's novel are a major attraction for thousands of tourists each year. However, may I point out that Count Dracula is not buried in the cemetery of the abbey. He is a fictional character. This does not seem to matter twice a year when thousands of "Goths" descend on the town for "Goth weekends". Some of these visitors were even sleeping in the cemetery at the abbey. The local police force soon put a stop to this strange activity.

Whitby Abbey.

The 199 steps from Whitby town up to the Abbey.

There is so much to do in this area I knew that we would both enjoy our time here. Hopefully we would not be moving on soon. To be honest I would be quite happy to spend the last 7 years of my military career in North Yorkshire.

Nick and myself were working well as a team in the communications centre and he was to prove responsible for me spending many wasted hours trying to hit a little ball a long way into a small hole. Golf was Nicks sport and he was very good at it. It just so happened that RAF Fylingdales had a golf society. In had an agreement with Whitby Golf Course that the members of the society could use the course at a much reduced payment. Fylingdales was allocated 12 tickets for the society members to use on any weekday. Membership of this group was only £5 per month. Nick decided it would be the right thing to do if we joined. Once that was done I needed to buy some sticks and anything else that was associated with the past-time. After a visit to the golf professional at the club I was soon fully equiped with everything required along with a few items that I had not thought off. The trolley was, as he said, "an essential" so who was I to argue. It was not long before Nick and myself came off a night shift and headed for our first game. Nick explained the handicap system and it appeared that he played off a very low number. This meant that I was given some 16 shots head start on him. I thought to myself arrogantly that a head start for me over the 18 holes would make me a winner before hitting anything. Toss of the coin gave Nick the right to start. He stepped up and "addressed" the ball. With a perfect back-swing he struck the ball and off it shot in a straight line down the fairway. "Well, that seems easy enough" I said. I tried to emulate his actions, swung the club back and instantly missed the ball. "That's 3 off the tee" he said. After another couple of swipes I actually hit the thing and it trundled about 30 yards along the grass. The hole that was to become my "Nemesis" was the 7th. Five times I tried to hit a ball across the valley at the start of that hole and failed every time. After several hours of laughter and frustration we finally completed the 18 holes. Basically I was rubbish and Nick had given me a sound thrashing but I was totally hooked on the game.

The dreaded 7th at Whitby golf course.

This one-sided contest was to happen on a regular basis while Nick was still with us and every time I never even got close to beating him.

John Boe arrived after his initial trade training at Cosford. John had no interest in golf, his sports being more of the physical type like football. Being a Leading Aircraftman he needed to achieve his trade ability tests (TAT's) before being let loose on the equipment unsupervised.

It was fast approaching the 18th birthday of Nick and his family back in Fleetwood had arranged the appropriate celebrations to mark the event. All in the communication centre were invited to attend. Most of us who were not working travelled to the west coast for what turned out to be a great weekend. Even the technician types, Steve Mcloud, Dan Hardwicke and Dave Holmes joined us. Nicks mother arranged places to rest our heads for the night. The one thing that I will always remember was our taxi's from the hotel to the venue of the party. Being a group of 6 we needed two vehicles. Leaving the reception lobby of the hotel we stepped outside to find the cars waiting for us were brand new Lada 1600 saloons. After being in a Lada, once while serving with Les Mann I knew they were somewhat uncomfortable. In we jumped. I was in the back and decided to light up a cigarette (*prior to the days when all smokers are classed as disgusting types*) I decided to open the window to let the smoke out and as I turned the handle for the window it came off in my hand. I did not have the heart to tell the driver I had broken his new taxi so just slid the offending handle under his seat. At least we left him a reasonable tip so I did not feel very guilty about it.

It was not long after this milestone in Nicks life that he was posted away to one of my old stomping grounds, No 6 Signals Unit, RAF Rudloe Manor. Farewell Nick it was a pleasure working alongside you. This meant that my future rounds of 18 would be as a solo player. I did try and get Dave Stewart interested but his thing was archery! He would spend hours on the grass opposite his married quarter doing a fine impression of Robin Hood. I decided he needed a nickname and henceforth he was referred to as "Twang" Stewart. It was now September 1988 and every spare minute was spent trying to hit a little ball in a straight line. I soon got into the routine of playing the first 7 and then calling into the White House hotel for a couple of pints before continuing. This surprisingly did help my swing to improve slightly.

Along came the replacement for Nick and this time it was somebody with a few years experience behind him. Doug Smith was a quietly spoken "Geordie lad". He settled in and was to become not just a workmate but a good friend. Doug and his wife Ann moved into the married quarters which meant I had a new drinking partner. Before long he was also accompanying me around the golf course. As he was also new to the game I felt I might actually win a few rounds. That was another mistake, he took to the game immediately and was soon putting me in my place. Our rounds become a regular event with the obligitory pause on the 7th green for a few beers. Ann wasted no time in getting a job in the same hotel as Elaine and after a few months she and Doug had decided to enter the property market. I wondered if I was going to lose my golfing & drinking partner but there was no need to worry. They bought a nice little place in the village of Staithes which is about 10 miles along the coast from Whitby. Both of them had full driving licence but only the single car. To overcome any transport problems Doug bought himself a little 50cc moped to get to Whitby for him golfing. If he had a few pints whilst spoiling a good walk he would leave this tiny machine in my garage and either use public transport or wait for Ann to finish work and pick him up. It was the perfect arrangement for everybody. On one occasion we convinced Elaine and Ann to "caddy" for us and we promised to pay for a lunch/drink after the seven holes. It was not the best of days with strong winds and driving rain. As we approached the 8th tee they looked at each other and just walked off. Obviously, not the game for them. Things were going perfectly and this was proving to be one of the best postings we could have had. Career wise I had so far been given two annual assessments from Rod & Harry. 7,8,8 and 8,7,7 with highly recommended much

pprieciated and dare I say deserved. Both Elaine and myself would be more
an happy to stay here for the rest of our days.

hn had reached the required level of knowledge and professionalism by now
d was promoted to Senior Aircraftman. Instantly he was placed on another
ift. Well done John even if you did spend a night in the custody of Whitby
olice station.

s with most postings there is always the individual who will end up being "the
y in the ointment". Mine was a Flight Sergeant Scopie. His name was Dave
arle. For some unknown reason he seemed to take an instant dislike to me. Out
f the blue somebody decided that RAF Fylingdales needed to have an exercise.
s I was on days off the call came from work that we all had to attend in our
PM's (or cabbage suits as they were fondly known). Having found this
othing hidden under the bed I dressed accordingly. I was waiting with the rest
f the commcen lads for our Wallace Arnold transport when this individual
pproached me and said "Where are your puttees, Corporal?" I replied that they
ere in my pocket.

puttee, also spelled puttie, is the name, adapted from the <u>Hindi</u> paṭṭī, bandage (<u>Skt.</u> paṭṭa, strip
cloth), for a covering for the lower part of the leg from the ankle to the knee, alternatively
own as: legwraps, leg bindings, winingas, or wickelbander. They consist of a long narrow piece
cloth wound tightly, and spirally round the leg, and serving to provide both support and
otection.

e then proceeded to tell me that he was charging me with being "improperly
essed". I pointed out that everybody at the bus-stop was improperly dressed as
e were all wearing civilian coats over our uniforms. This we had to do when
avelling on the bus. Apparently it made us look like civilians going on a bus
ip. He was not having any of it and officially charged me. Everybody thought
is mad. Thankfully this charge was instantly dismissed by higher authority.
obody could take the whole saga seriously and it became an ongoing joke for
everal months. Dave Karle was never a thorn in my side again.

s we were not getting any younger Elaine decided it was time for me to get a
ll driving licence, doing it properly this time and having driving lessons. I had
good source for buying a car. Every weekend in the summer a family came to
hitby to spend time in their caravans. These characters used the White House
otel and I had got to know them well. They always stopped off in Ruswarp
llage and bought what seemed like a ton of "pork scratchings" to share around
 the Sunday lunchtime sessions. They owned a second-hand car dealership in
uddersfield. It was no problem for them to find me a set of wheels. A light
ue Opel Ascona was brought along for my inspection. £800 changed hands
d I now had 4 wheels added to the collection in the garage. Lessons paid for

with a recognised instructor and I set about getting through the dreaded driving test. In-between my official lessons Doug would accompany me in the Ascona to get more experience. I had less than half a dozen trips with my instructor when he decided to put me through the test. Apparently I had a good road-sense. In anticipation of things to come I parted with my beloved motorcycle to what I hoped was a good home. The day of my test came and off I went with the instructor in his little Renault 5. In my opinion everything went well but the examiner decided that I was a failure. It seems that I did not show due consideration to a pedestrian who was about 30 metres away from a pedestrian crossing. To me this was rubbish as the person in question would have had to be an Olympic sprinter to beat me to the crossing. Not in a happy place I expressed my disgust with him and got my instructor to take me home.

One week later I was given what proved to be my final annual assessment. I must have been squeaky clean in the last year because Rod & Harry thought I deserved 8,8,8 with special recommendation for promotion. This was the highest anybody could achieve so maybe my attempt at being a "model airman" over the last 4 years had paid off. Alas though as I had been given a reprimand for not following a direct order my conduct was only given as "very good". Thanks to Flight Sergeant Karle, no Long Service & Good Conduct medal for this veteran. Another attempt at the driving test was booked. I knew that if I ended up with the same examiner I was "screwed". For Elaine though I would give it my best shot and keep my mouth shut. Things just got hectic from this point. Going into work on a wonderful summers' day, Rod gave me the bad news that I had been posted. No 3 Maritime Headquarters, Plymouth would be expecting me. Another tour with the RAuxAF was the last thing I wanted. To make things worse my date of posting was the day after I would be taking my driving test, for the second time. If I blew it this time we were truly stuffed with no transport at all. I am not going to say I was nervous on my test but if I had failed again it was going to cause massive problems. Doug agreed to be a great mate and if the worst happened he would drive the car down to Plymouth, returning on the train. Elaine packed everything and I loaded up the car ready for the trip. Test time came and off to the test centre in Whitby I went in the Renault alongside an incredibly nervous instructor. For the full 30 minutes of that trauma my hands would not stop shaking. Getting back to the test centre my examiner announced, "congratulations, you have passed". If I had been the religious type I would have given a massive "hallelujah". I had never been so relieved and gave him a vigorous handshake. I now had a piece of paper that allowed me to drive 4-wheels, legally.

t was with total sadness that we closed the front door of our little house in Derwent Road for the last time. We had been in Whitby for 2 years and 2 months. Every moment of that time had been memorable for all the right reasons. Farewell, North Yorkshire, we will return one day.

My thanks go out to all at Royal Air Force Fylingdales that I served alongside:

Rod Mclennan & Harry McMenemy. (Boss senior & junior)

Doug Smith, Nick Matley, John Boe, Mick Meechan, Dave Stewart, Dan Hardwicke, Steve McCloud, Dave Holmes, Darren Ellam. (the working lads).

Next stop: No 3 Maritime Headquarters Unit, Royal Air Force Mount Batten.

Chapter 4.

No 3 Maritime Headquarters Unit – Mount Batten.

September 1989 – April 1990.

(Back with the part-timers).

Whilst driving down to the south coast of Devon, I was wondering who I had managed to upset this time. Due to my previous time in London I knew this posting was not going to be of any benefit to my promotion prospects.

Elaine and I were both settled and happy in Whitby. She had enjoyed her role in the Royal Hotel and I was more than content with working at Fylingdales. Yet again she would have to start hunting for new employment and settle down again. Someone at the Personnel Management Centre, RAF Innsworth had obviously taken a personal dislike to me. What confused me more was the fact that I was posted to Fylingdales because the establishment levels had changed with the three Auxiliary units. Each one was now manned with just the one sergeant. Why then was I being sent as a corporal to 3 MHU, Plymouth?

Turning up at Royal Air Force Station Mount Batten was like travelling back in time. It was a small station covering a small piece of land on the coastline of Plymouth. Right away I could notice that this place had seen better days. Everything was looking rather grubby and neglected. It had in former times been a highly active station but those days were long gone.

"On the 1st of October 1928, following re-building, the old Cattewater seaplane station was opened as Royal Air Force Station Mount Batten. The main reason for the station was to provide a base for flying boats to defend south-west England.

The station was named after Captain Batten, a civil war commander who defended the area at the time.

With the start of the second world war there was an increase in operational flying from Mount Batten. It was a major target for several German air raids which achieved the destruction of one of the hangers and a Short Sunderland on the 28th of November 1940.

Short Sunderland of 10 Sqn at Mount Batten.

t the end of hostilities the station became a maintenance unit. The role of the ation was changed again at the of the 1950s and it became the Marine Craft 'raining School. In 1961 it became the main base for the marine branch. This ontinued until the marine branch was closed in 1986".

 was now September 1989 and all that was left on the station were 2 resident nits. School of Survival and No 3 Maritime Headquarters Unit (RAuxAF).

igning in at the guardroom we drove down to the family's office to collect ome keys for a new house. He was a welcoming civilian who proceeded to ick up several bunches of keys to properties for us to look at. We followed him ff the base to the married quarters in Plymstock, just a couple of miles away. he first one he showed me was in reasonable condition so I shook his hand, igned the appropriate paperwork and took a bunch of keys from him. Just like 1ount Batten this patch of houses were in a somewhat run down condition. here was a mixture of civilian, RAF and Navy family's resident on the site. lowever the allocated married quarter was clean enough for us to move in traight away. There was none of the usual facilities like a NAAFI shop or ocial centre available so any social life would be in the civilian environment.

ur first night in the new home was spent sleeping fully clothed as the removal an from Whitby would not be arriving until the next day. Prior to an extremely ncomfortable night of sleep we wandered over to the nearest public house Drakes Drum) for something to eat and a few drinks. The Drakes Drum was ot one of the best establishments we had ever been in. I could compare it nfavourably with the local we had in Colindale a few years earlier. The only ifference was that your shoes did not stick to the carpet when you walked in.

Our belongings arrived early the next morning and the task of unpacking it could start. Elaine had become an expert at packing/unpacking by this time and had a well-rehearsed and organised system. In order not to get in her way I left her to go through the routine, she preferred it that way. I would spend the morning doing my official arrival at my new station. Mount Batten being such a small place this task was completed in no time at all. I left 3 MHU for my last port of call and finding it I was surprised because it was just an old wooden building with 2 rows of offices. I wandered into the adjutant's office and introduced myself. This "shack" was the workplace to 4 regular staff in the administration office and a single regular instructor with his own training office I knew the instructor at once, John Rafferty had been in basic training at the same time as me some 17 years earlier. It was obvious that his conduct up to this time had been of a higher standard than mine, he had made it to the Sergeants Mess. As we all sat around having a cup of coffee I only had one question for them all, "Why am I here". None of them could come up with an answer. Everybody just accepted that there must be a perfectly logical reason for my arrival but all accepted that none of us understood the logic of it.

Anyway, I decided not to pursue the matter and just get on with whatever my job was supposed to be. John said that he had nowhere enough work to occupy his own time so finding stuff for the two of us to do was going to be difficult. It was decided that I would basically sit around and pretend to be doing something important. After all I was still getting paid for doing nothing. We both agreed that there must have been a clerical error somewhere and when it was discovered I would be moved away quickly. I did find something useful to occupy a bit of time when the weather was kind. My 9 iron and putter were getting some use on the grass next to our building most days of the week.

Royal Air Force Station Mount Batten.

laine was not going to be stuck in the house all day and set about finding
uitable employment. Job application went off to the Mayflower Hotel in
lymouth. Within 10 days of our arrival she was back in the hospitality business
nd slowly finding her feet as a chambermaid in a much larger hotel than the
ne in Whitby. Plymouth had one positive point and that was the shopping
acilities. After the somewhat limited choice in Whitby this town was a
hopper's paradise. Christmas came and went with the usual lack of celebration,
routine we had now got accustomed too. The unit Christmas party was
omething that I had to attend as the adjutant was very persuasive. He said it
ould be better as our attendance would swell the numbers in attendance. The
uxiliary manpower was about 50 personnel but it was expected that less than
alf would make the effort to show up. Nothing like the London unit where if
ne word "drink" was mentioned there was a 100% showing. However, fate took
hand in my attendance. On the night of the party I had been detailed to carry
ut the role of duty NCO for the station. This entailed sitting in the guardroom
ith an airman from 1700 until 0800 the next morning. It would be 13 hours of
necking the identity of anybody coming on the station. Apart from the
nembers of 3MHU that turned up for the party we never opened the gate to any
ther living soul until those working the next day showed up. Due to boredom I
andered down to the party for a pint of beer. The adjutant was happy as I was
omebody else for him to have a chat with.

oth of us felt uncomfortable about living on the housing estate in Plymstock as
was going through a spate of break-ins. These crimes were usually committed
hen the occupants were away on leave. Being old houses the security systems
ere to say the least "basic". The front door was secured with a yale lock and
othing more. All the windows were metal framed with a flimsy single latch.
ot much of a deterrent to any would be burglar. This situation continued for
everal weeks until the culprit was apprehended by the local constabulary. The
ieving git was the son of an RAF corporal who was the resident General
uties (GD) in the guardroom. This individual was furnishing his son with the
ddress of all those who were on annual leave. After this, normal life was
esumed.

nother thing that we noticed on the estate was that every time a Royal Navy
nip left Plymouth there was a sudden surge in unknown vehicles outside
arious houses. A large proportion were tatty white vans. The house opposite
urs had one such arrival and prominent in the kitchen window was a box of
ashing powder with the brand name OMO. I will leave you to draw the

connection between these two things. I had heard about the "Old Man Out" happening in some areas but never thought I would ever witness it happening.

Life continued in a hum-drum routine with Elaine working and me doing absolutely nothing apart from practicing my golf swing. Even the training weekends made no difference and if I had not bothered to turn up nobody would have noticed or cared. Winter was rolling by and we decided it was time to make a trip over to the cemetery in Germany in the springtime. It had been a few years since our last trip to Rheindahlen. Ferry bookings were made for the end of April.

Halfway through March and I enthusiastically (as usual) rolled into work. Doing the usual chatting and drinking coffee with John, the adjutant asked if he could see me in his office. Maybe they have found a job for me at last? I mean I had not done anything at all so it was not for a dressing down. "Take a seat, Lee". Plonking myself in the comfy chair he just came straight out with it, "Congratulations on your promotion". I was stunned into silence but once I regained my composure I said, "Are you sure, Sir". As I had been given my formal warning less than 4 years earlier I did not believe him at all. "Really" he responded. Leaving his office in a somewhat dazed state I thanked him. John was waiting in the corridor for me and asked what was going on. I explained to him and he went white with shock. Not because of my promotion but as there were now 2 Sergeants on the unit, one of us would be leaving. His shock soon turned to depression. He explained that his children were in school in Plymouth. One of them was in her final exam's year. A move at this time was the last thing he wanted. He asked if he were posted would I take it in his place so that he could stay. "That all depends on where it is" was my response. He really wanted to stay at Mount Batten for at least another year. I did not need to discuss this with Elaine as she would really be anywhere rather than Plymstock.

It transpired that when I was posted to 3 MHU it was to fill the role of communications instructor. However, because I was on the formal warning promotion of any type was not possible until a set time after that formal warning. I had to do the minimum time before promotion. I wonder if the adjutant was made aware of this upon my arrival 6 months earlier!. Getting home that evening I explained to Elaine what had happened and she was delighted, not just for the promotion but for the chance to move away. Naturally we would not now be taking the trip we had booked to Germany.

It was only a few days until the posting for Sgt John Rafferty came in. He was posted to No 81 Signals Unit (N) at RAF Kinloss, Scotland. On the mainland of e British Isles that is about the furthest you can get from Plymouth. 650 miles ading North. Would I swop with John. It did not take long to decide. I jumped the chance. High Frequency radio communications or instructing part-timers, hich would any radio lover choose? This is where I said farewell to those that had come across during the last few months and get moving again.

he one memory of this place that will remain with me is golf related. Mount atten had its own golf team (4 of them) and they took part in a league of the ilitary bases in the South-West. A match against RAF Chivenor was due but he of the team would not be available. Now I had been seen at work improving y chipping & putting skills. The captain of the team asked me if I could make the numbers against Chivenor. I decided to give it a go and not let the station wn. Off we went on a freezing morning to Chivenor and prepared for 2 lots of ball. The captain decided to partner me in one team. We won the toss and he ve me the honour of being first to tee off. First hole was a 300yd+ par 4. This eant I needed to give it a hefty drive. Taking my 3 wood out of the bag I did e usual warm up swings. Then addressing the ball like a professional I swung e club back and let rip. "Crack", I hit the ball clean centre. It went about 6 feet ithout lifting at all, hit the ladies tee marker, shot up and whistled at eye-level st my head. Final resting position for my first shot was around 100 yards hind the first tee. Not the best of starts and it just went further downhill from at point. I bet the captain wished he had just forfeited the game and not thered with me at all.

day in 2021 little evidence of the Royal Air Force base remains apart from veral memorials, some aviation related road names, the main slipway and two pressive Grade II listed F-type aeroplane hangars dating from 1917.

RAF Mount Batten memorial.

Elaine got most of the packing in our AMQ done in record time and halfway through April 1990 we were heading North looking forward to a new adventure.

Farewell Plymouth. Next stop No 81 Signals Unit (N), Royal Air Force Kinloss, Morayshire, Scotland.

Chapter 5.
Royal Air Force Kinloss.
April 1990 – December 1991.
(Home of the "Mighty Hunter").

Travelling from the bottom to almost the top of the United Kingdom meant we would need an overnight stay somewhere. We decided to call in on my parents who had moved to Melrose in the borders. We had not seen much of them since our marriage 15 years ago. The two times we had met were the usual cold experiences. The usual outcome was me losing it totally with my mother. Having no idea of when we would arrive at Kinloss, our good friend and best man at the wedding in 1975 agreed to be a proxy for me and take over the married quarter. Dave Mitchell was already stationed there and working on the Nimrod simulators teaching the "growbags" how to communicate properly. "Growbag" was the name given to the aircrews of the Nimrod because they wore flying coveralls all the time. The pilots used to refer to them as "talking weight".

The night stop in Melrose was less traumatic than we both expected but Sam decided it safer to stay in his cat travel basket. I succeeded in attaining a first by not falling out with my mother. My father was his usual self, drinking Carlsberg special brew to excess. He was also prone to suffering from depression and this could lead to severe downers at any time. A few months earlier he had taken a disliking to the double glazing in the bungalow. Wandered around with a 12-bore shotgun and proceeded to remove several of the windows. After that little incident he spent several weeks in medical care, which seemed to have had a beneficial result and calmed him down a bit.

During our 2 day drive, we were amazed at the difference in weather conditions. We left Plymouth in glorious sunshine with spring flowers out everywhere. Heading North on the A9 towards the Cairngorm mountains we were greeted with heavy snowfall and a temperature drop of about 8 degrees. Married quarter address in hand we turned up at our new home late in the morning. I could see Dave waiting outside. Elaine decided to stay in the car and keep Sam company, while I collected the keys. When I opened the front door I was almost knocked backwards by the smell of animal urine. The smell was worse than any CS gas chamber I had been forced to endure earlier in my career. As I walked in I felt like being sick. Into the living room and I could feel the wetness in the carpet.

All the doors and skirting boards were filthy. Opening the back door to the garden I was greeted by a totally disgusting sight. What was supposed to be a lawn was covered in piles of dog faeces. The fencing between this hovel and the adjoining married quarters was destroyed. That was enough for me and I did not even bother to look around the rest of the house. As I stormed out of the front door I let rip at Dave and used far too many expletives to express my anger. To this day I still regret that outburst because it was not his fault in any way. Not only had he been a good friend since our childhood days but he was doing us a favour by "marching in" on our behalf. It was a friendship that went back many years. Our careers started together with "square-bashing at Swinderby, trade training at Cosford and first operational postings to Lyneham. When Dave got married to Marie-Anne they went straight into the property market. This meant that he had never lived in any married quarters in his career.

When I got back to the car, Elaine could sense that things were not going smoothly. I looked at her and said: "that is disgusting and you are not living there". Next move was to sign in on the base and around to the family's officer. Because this was our tenth married quarter, we both understood the system employed by a lot of the family's officers. Each time you move out of an RAF married quarter, a report on the condition of the property is placed on file. The cleaner you left it meant that at some stations you would get allocated something a little below a decent standard. This way they knew that when you left it would be in a much better condition than when you "marched in". Elaine had always left a spotless property so there were not blemishes on our record.

As I walked into the family's office I decided to keep a cool head. The first person I came across was one of his assistants who asked if she could help me. "I would like to see the family's officer, NOW, please". When she enquired the nature of my request I just responded with: "It is about the shithole he allocated to me this morning". Asking who I was she proceeded to shuffle several pieces f paper and replied: "I see you had a proxy who accepted the accommodation s acceptable" at this point I pointed out that it was not fit for any human abitation. Picking up the telephone she called her superior and asked me to go to his office. Behind a cluttered desk was a somewhat scruffy civilian with a cigarette hanging from the corner of his mouth. He took one glance at me and said: "Corporal Hammond, your nominated proxy accepted the married quarter, o you are stuck with it". My reply stunned him totally, "It is Sergeant now and do not accept it, either you get me something up to a liveable standard or I will et an interview with the Station Commander, with you in attendance" After pluttering he explained that there was a vacant house on the South Side narried quarters that may prove to be in an acceptable condition. "Right, let's o and have a look now". After a glance at his watch he said it will have to wait s it was his lunch time. This was where my cool head ceased operating. I let rip t him and explained that after driving for two days and having my wife and cat a the car I was not in a good mood. I stared at him and explained that when he ot back from his lunch, I would still be in his office but this time with the tation Commander. He finally saw sense and unwillingly agreed to doing his ob and have a late lunch.

Ve followed him to a collection of much newer married quarters which all ppeared to be in somewhat better structural condition than the older buildings n the North Side. As we went through the front door of a 2 bedroom house it ras amazing at the difference compared to an hour earlier. The whole house ras spotless and had just been fully re-decorated. The back garden had solid anel fencing down both sides. At the bottom of the garden were fields as far as ie eye could see. I asked why he did not offer us this one in the first place. A uestion to which he was unable to give any sort of answer. After signing all the elevant paperwork he handed me the keys. Away he went, muttering something nder his breath about troublemakers. All sorted Elaine and Sam could now nally get out of the car and stretch their legs. Most important thing on the list ow is contact the removals company and let them know the change of address or delivery. After unloading the car we left Sam to explore his new home and rent into Findhorn, just over 2 miles away for a much deserved meal and drink. nce the car was unloaded it was time to relax. The last two days had been hard rork and I had a few days off before having to report to my new place of mployment, 81 Signals Unit.

1y new unit had not been long in existence but I was looking forward to the nallenge and it involved my true love of radio communications.

rior to 1980 each radar station, flying unit and command had its own high equency (HF) radio services for communications with its own flying assets.

Some 20 years earlier it was realised that these networks would in the future not be able to provide a reliable all round cover, particularly when it was announced that the Royal Navy aircraft carrier fleet was to be phased out. This meant that the Royal Air Force would be required to provide the air cover for the fleet. Then in the early 1970's it was decided that Strike Command would set up a new communications network utilising modern radio equipment. In February 1977 work commenced on Headquarters 81Signals Unit, RAF Bampton Castle. This was to be the receiver site and the work was completed in November 1978. On 1st November 1979 Bampton Castle became the operational home of HQ 81SU and 81 SU detachment (South) to provide an Integrated High Frequency Radio service for all Strike Command stations and units.

The northern detachment 81 SU detachment (North) was situated on the operational base of Kinloss. This would provide geographic diversity and survivability in case of any future conflict. The transmitter sites for these two units were at RAF Chelveston (South) and RAF Milltown (North).

These two units are responsible for providing strategic, long haul frequency radio communications to all military personnel in need of their services. This was achieved using the Strike Command Integrated Communications System (STCICS), and the Maritime Aeronautical Telecommunications Organisation System (MATELO). These systems provide high frequency (HF) voice communications to RAF aircraft, RN vessels, tactical communications units along with any other unit that had a requirement for high frequency voice communications. It was also available to other military organisations including the Air Training Corps squadrons for radio familiarisation training.

With the allocation of the callsign "Architect" 81 SU provided voice communications with any Royal Air Force aircraft flying anywhere in the world. This is possible by the constant monitoring of 10 guard frequencies. These are predetermined frequencies that are permanently monitored by the staff of the 2 detachments. Both units also provide airfield colour states and barometric pressure settings. Both sets of information are broadcast at predetermined and published times 24 hours a day. Agencies who require a more detailed weather broadcast can receive such information for any airfield worldwide by simply calling on one of the guard frequencies. The STICICS operator can then provide the requested information within seconds. The facility to get instant contact with any base was also available via a telephone network. The main objective is to provide a reliable communications system for flight safety. The recognised Distress & Rescue frequencies are monitored continually by 81 SU personnel.

efore turning up for the usual arrival procedure, I had to ensure that my niform was cleaned and ironed, a haircut was also needed. My 7 months in lymouth had seen standards drop off to a level not acceptable in the "real" Air orce. Going in on my first day was more of a challenge than I expected and I m glad I took the car. 81 SU was in a secure compound on the far side of the irfield. Once on Kinloss station it was a long drive passing rows of Nimrod ircraft and the main runway.

Nimrod MR2 (The Mighty Hunter).

soon became obvious that walking to work was not an option. I parked up and fter showing identity went into the administration office to introduce myself. hose working in there were a couple of Senior Aircraftwomen, 1 Corporal and Sergeant. With the usual welcomes out of the way I was taken to meet the /arrant Officer. His was a warm welcome and he explained that I would be uty Signals Master for one of the 4 shifts under his command. This would volve shift work of 2 days, 2 nights. I was more than happy with this as I ways preferred working on shift rather than doing the boring Monday – Friday ay work. In my opinion working on shift was more of a family atmosphere and astly more relaxed regarding the rank structure. It was explained that the fficer Commanding would interview me once my arrival procedure had been ompleted. It was at this point that I mentioned the arrival may take some time, inloss was a large base and I had no idea where anything was. He then got the orporal on days to take me around the base in our own unit transport and get it one in no time at all. My longest stop was at the Sergeants Mess. I had to varn in" which means that from that point I am a member and liable to the sual monthly mess bill. Once this was all over we drove back to the unit on the cenic route so I could learn where everything was.

I was then given a tour of the facility and it was pure coincidence that the shift currently working on days was the one I would be responsible for. I was taken into the operations room and firstly introduced to my Corporals, Phil Bayles, Nige Hocking and one other whose name I just cannot remember. There were some seven or eight operators in the team who were carrying out their duties to the high level of professionalism that I expected. There was one who was instantly recognisable to me. Nick Matley, my old golfing partner from Fylingdales was amongst them. It was good to catch up with him again and I knew that visits to Forres golf course would be forthcoming.

After that it was in to see the Commanding Officer. He was a young Flight Lieutenant, engineering officer. His approach was totally relaxed and explained "You run your crew how you see fit and keep them out of any trouble". His knowledge of radio communications was to say the least, somewhat limited. It was refreshing to be working for a commissioned officer who would leave the trained experts alone. He also explained that I was responsible for discipline & morale, I was to leave the actual working of the systems to the other ranks. Oh well! I accepted that being promoted had its negatives as well as positives of a good pay rise and better pension. Once I started I noticed that this team had no problems with either discipline or morale. It was obvious that there was not a lot for me to do except authorise leave and hand out the stand-downs, which we referred to as "gash time off".

I had only been in my position for a month when I paid my second visit to the Sergeants Mess. This was to say farewell to my friend Roger Scutt. He was a crew member on the Avro Shackleton which had recently crashed during a training exercise. There is no need to go in-depth about the incident as it is fully covered in an earlier chapter. My first visit for an evening drink in the Mess bar was a few days later and I walked away somewhat disappointed. I approached the bar and placed my order. Whilst waiting for it to be poured I sat down on one of the bar stools. "You're a brave man" said the barman. After enquiring the nature of his comment, he pointed out the bar stool was the favourite of a Chief Technician (*name forgotten*). He then explained that several of the living in members had put claim to all the bar stools. Not to cause any offence I took my drink to a table and decided to just observe what went on. "Growbags" came in and left with pints in hand. They tended to keep together in the snooker room or television rooms as they were "improperly dressed" in the issued flying coveralls. A few others came in and sat at the tables chatting amongst themselves. One elderly member entered and promptly sat on his bar stool. I later learned that he was one of the many who lived-in permanently due to failed marriages or other personal reasons. Leaving after about an hour I felt

omewhat deflated. For years I had really looked forward to being a member of
his somewhat elite club. The whole experience had turned out to be somewhat
f an anti-climax. From now on I would do my best to use either the local
ublic houses or if I could get away with it the Junior Ranks NAAFI bar. At
ast these would have a livelier atmosphere than the Sergeants Mess. For the
ext year my only visits were to pay my monthly mess bill.

ack at home, Elaine was going through the usual job searching routine. This
me with no success. There was not a lot of employment locally apart from the
inloss and Lossiemouth air bases. There were most certainly no large
mployers in the hospitality business. She soon resigned herself to being a
ousewife for the duration of this posting.

lot had changed in the 10 years since me reaching the dizzy heights of
orporal. Now in the modern Royal Air Force, training was needed to act like a
roper Non-Commissioned Officer. Until I had completed this training I was
fficially an "acting" Sergeant. The first course for me to attend would be
eneral Service Training (GST) at RAF Hereford followed by Further Training
T) at RAF Locking. It was all vastly different from the days of getting a
romotion and carrying on as before.

rriving at Hereford, I had no idea what to expect over the one week period.
his was all new to me. The training package was set-up to teach us leadership
ills and problem solving. An emphasis on "team-work" was drilled into us.
asically it came down to: "Look after your subordinates and they will look
ter you". There were a lot of laughs and debate about problems solving
xercises like, getting over a stream using some planks of wood and a lot of
pe. We all got on well and achieved the required standards to gain a creditable
ass.

With that one behind me it was a short stay at home before heading South again this time to the Communications School at RAF Locking. This would not be a new experience as most of the civilian instructing staff were already known to me, from my days when the training school was located at RAF Cosford. FT courses from my experience were basically just a get-together of fellow communications staff and were very laid-back affairs. There were 11 of us and apart from our two instructors they were all new faces to me. Instructing us were Les Binns & the legend of RAF communications, Mr Reg Howarth. It was great to meet up with them again after so many years.

It turned out to be 2 weeks of enjoyment with the occasional session of learning thrown in as well. The staff, most of whom I knew stitched me up on the first week. Locking being a training camp held a Station Commanders parade on Friday mornings before training started. I was informed that I had been selected as the parade senior NCO and was expected to do a good job. In all honesty I knew that they expected me to make a right "pigs-ear" of the whole event. As the last time I was on a proper parade dated back to 1972 when I passed out of my basic training at Swinderby, I expected everything to go wrong.

Turning up on the parade square at the appointed time I was amazed at how many trainees were all waiting for the circus to begin. Going to the front of the parade I noticed a Corporal with the smartest appearance of all in attendance. I asked him what his trade was and after he explained he was General Duties (GD). He was involved in these parades every week working alongside the Station Warrant Officer. I formulated a plan to save my upcoming embarrassment. I asked if he would stand beside me and tell me what commands I had to give and when to give them. I also explained that it had been 17 years since I last spent any time on a parade square. "I will be right beside you, Sarge" was his reply. The next 30 minutes went like clockwork and as they all marched off I felt a massive sense of relief that it was over. Arriving at the communications school that morning I wandered up to the office, opened the door, stuck my head in and said: "up yours, you lot, it all went perfectly". To show the appreciation I had for my new Corporal friend I delivered a six pack of beers to the guardroom for his personal consumption.

The end of week one arrived and there was no way I was driving all the way up to Kinloss just to turn around and come back so it was to be a weekend in Weston-Super-Mare. Others on the course decided not to travel home so at least there were a few of us to do the obligatory "pub-crawl". I had never been to this part of the world before so the seaside town was all new to me. Although this own claimed to be a seaside resort it was not actually anywhere near the sea. It s on the Bristol Channel and at low tide the town is some 1 mile away from any water. When the tide is in there are sandy beaches but when the tide is out it reveals a thick mud as far as the eye can see. A good weekend was had by all of us but I would not bother going back again. Like all seaside towns in England, Weston had seen better days. Since the start of value sunshine holidays to Spain back in the 1960s the traditional seaside towns of England had seen a massive drop in visitors.

Within the confines of RAF Locking were hundreds of apple trees. Apparently these apples were collected annually by a large brewing company for the manufacture of cider. Instructions to the personnel were that they were not to be picked by anyone but cider company employees. However I decided that the ones on the ground were easy pickings and I would transport some of them home and have a go at home-brew. After breakfast on the Sunday I collected as many as I could cram into the car boot. Every one of these was what I classed as windfall so I had not broken any rules.

The second week of the course proceeded with no mishaps and we all said our farewells to Reg & Les. It had been good to meet them again but now it was time to head 550 miles back home.

Now that both the training courses were out of the way I could concentrate on maintaining the morale of my staff. It was my intention to just let what was, in my eyes, running smoothly alone and not change anything. This proved a sensible move because in my time there I never had any problems with any of my team. Every now and then I just could not resist sitting at one of the operator positions and converse with the occasional Hercules (Fat Albert) aircraft en-route back to Lyneham. There were times when the units Officer Commanding would come into the operations room and catch me doing this. He would just give me a glare. He just accepted that every now then I would have as he called it "a little play with the kit". The months were passing by and I was enjoying every moment at Kinloss.

I had made good use of my apples collected while at Locking. The home-made cider was ready. I have never liked it so Elaine was to be my chief taster and critic. Half a pint was dispensed and she sipped somewhat sheepishly. Result was that she thought it a particularly good effort. The rest of the glass was finished. 2 hours later she was in the back of an ambulance on her way to Inverness hospital. The alcohol level in this "hootch" was around 10% abv and with her being diabetic her system had not taken kindly to it. After that experience she decided not to finish of the several gallons I had left. This I passed on to Phil Bayles as his wife Avril was a cider drinker as well. This was yet another mistake because when I was dropping Phil at home after a day shift we noticed Avril and a few other wives in the street. All I can say is that they were all in high spirits. That was the first and last time I have ever made cider at home.

Our workload was soon to see a massive increase because on the 2nd of August 1990, the armed forces of Saddam Hussein, leader of Iraq had seen fit to invade the neighbouring state of Kuwait. A coalition of armed forces from 35 nations was formed. Over the next few months there was a build-up of the coalition forces in Saudi Arabia. The leaders of the western world had decided to take back the country for the Kuwaiti people. Once all the pieces were in place on the chessboard on the 17th of January 1991 Operation Granby commenced, with the Royal Air Force playing a major part.

Operation Granby, commonly abbreviated Op Granby, was the code name given to the British military operations during the 1991 Gulf War. 53,462 members of the British Armed Forces were deployed during the conflict. The total cost of operations was £2.434 billion of which at least £2.049 billion was paid for by other nations such as Kuwait and Saudi Arabia. £200 million of equipment was lost or written off. 47 British servicemen lost their lives during the conflict. Liberation of Kuwait was achieved on 28th of February 1991.

Although it was busy at work due to the build-up to conflict, I had to decide who would be working on Christmas day. My plan was: all the married personnel with children would have the day off as a stand-down, all the single personnel and those without children would work alongside me. All those that worked hristmas would then be given New Year's Day off as a stand-down. To my urprise there was a 100% agreement. Getting any stand-down was rare now as e build-up in the Gulf was gaining pace all the time.

was now the last days of 1990 and I received the sad news that my great friend Fylingdales, Harry McMenemy has died at Christmas. He was eating mething and it became stuck. Taken into hospital things got worse as this cident had caused a blood clot which went to his brain. Harry was only 39 years d. He had left behind his wife Alberta along with children Julie and David. To e this was a hammer blow. Roger had left us earlier in the year and now Harry. oth were in the prime of life. Alberta gave me all the details of the funeral and r me it was a trip back to Whitby. I always intended to return to this lovely town it not in these circumstances. I will always remember that fateful day in January 991 because it was the coldest I have ever been. The church service was carried it with a fantastic turn-out from the Fylingdales staff. It was then up to Whitby metery to say farewell to a good friend.

Last resting place for Harry in Whitby cemetery.

he drive home after the funeral was to take several hours because of constant owstorms and strong winds. It was the first time in my life that I had been ared driving a car. A few weeks later, Alberta phoned me to tell me that the inistry of Defence had given her 6 weeks to vacate the married quarter. It was st another sign how much the ministry does not care about servicemen and their milies.

ith the festive season out of the way, things started to get even more hectic and the 17th of January 1991 the battle to evict the Iraqi forces commenced. For e next 5 weeks "Architect" was working flat out. When the conflict came to end the 28th of February we had weathered the storm and I was proud of my whole team. Over the next few weeks, aircraft returned to their UK & German bases apart from the 8 Tornado aircraft losses, 5 of which were lost on combat missions It was all over and some sort of normality was returning to the workplace. I fo one was amazed that the British armed forces managed to achieve what they dic because ever since the fall of the Berlin wall some 2 years earlier, our military budget had been massively cut and not only were the numbers of personnel being slashed but aircraft were being scrapped and bases closed. The armed forces o the United Kingdom were the third largest contributors to the coalition. Ou friends from "across the pond" the United States had contributed 697,0(personnel. Saudi Arabia supplied 60,000+.

The system of allowing my capable Corporals to run everything resumed and just tried to make myself look busy if anybody came into the operations room. I was a cold February morning when the Officer Commanding entered and strod straight up to me. "You can Ski can't you Sarge". I replied in the positive as I hac done a ski course when in Germany. Ever since then Elaine and I have hit the slopes of various Austrian resorts most years. The conversation then led onto how busy we were and could I spare some bodies. As it was incredibly quiet I offerec him half of the bodies currently on shift. "Great" was his response. "See whc wants to come skiing". 4 volunteers stepped forward and we all bundled into the unit Sherpa mini-bus. I dropped them at station stores to collect ski equipmen and then went home to get my own kit. It was then to the Officers Married Quarte of my boss to collect his wife. We set off for the ski resort at The Lecht Ski Centre which was about a one hour drive away. The weather was awful. It was raining and the ski slopes were somewhat slushy. It was nothing like the dry powder snov you get in the Alps. After a few hours there were 7 very wet bodies heading back to base. Everybody seemed to enjoy it and the boss had now got the skiing bug. had spent several hours picking people up and trying to get them to master the basics of the snow-plough position with little success.

For the next few months everything was running like clockwork. Suddenly it wa brought to my attention that the High Frequency communications of the Roya Air Force were being put out to tender for civilian firms to take over. Yet more cuts to the defence budget of the nation. For me it was the final straw, time to hand in the uniform and see what civilian street had to offer. In no time at all we were looking to enter the property market and set down roots. Elaine was keen to do this as there was no chance of getting any employment while we remained in this part of Scotland. Because the Royal Air Force was being cut back at a rapic rate there were hundreds of former married quarters available for purchase by serving personnel. The areas available were all over the United Kingdom but we had decided if possible to stay in Scotland. Among those up for sale were abou

...0 former airman's married quarters in the town of Anstruther, Fife. We decided ...o go and have a look at what was on offer. Arriving in the town we had an instant ...king to the area and the houses seemed to be in a good state of repair. We both ...greed that an application to buy one needed to be put in. It was going to cost us ...st under £20,000 so first thing to do was arrange a mortgage. Being on a good ...te of pay at the time (£16,000) our first application with the Nationwide ...uilding Society was instantly accepted. It was now July 1991 and our hopes ...ere that it would all be sorted before November when the weather would take a ...own-turn. After about a month we received a letter stating that we had been ...ffered one of the Anstruther properties. 6 March Crescent, Cellardyke, ...nstruther was going to be our new home. Thankfully everything went smoothly ...d we were leaving our last airman's married quarter heading for "our home" in ...e middle of September. Now I had to apply for a Last Tour of Duty (LTD) and ...nish my 22 year contract at pastures new. The nearest RAF station to our new ...ome was RAF Leuchars. This was a flying unit across the River Tay. It was only ...5 miles from home and would be perfect for the commute to work. The ...aperwork was completed and now I had to hope there was a slot for me to fill.

...a the meantime as it was 160 miles from our new home to Kinloss I would have ...o move into the mess until a posting came through. I only really used the mess ...s somewhere to get some sleep in-between shifts. My social time revolved ...ound local public houses or the NAAFI with Phil and the rest of the crew. If ...ere was a formal function in the mess I would attend as I had already paid for ...t through my mess bill. My routine became mundane, working 2 days & 2 nights ...en heading home for a few days before doing it all again. Over the next 3 ...onths I went into automatic mode driving up and down the A9. When winter ...rived it was getting a lot more stressful and tiring doing that journey so often.

...nally, at the start of December my Last Tour of Duty was given to me. It was ...ot RAF Leuchars as I had wished but RAF Pitreavie Castle. It appeared the two ...ergeants at Leuchars were both happy and had no intention of moving ...oluntarily. Pitreavie Castle was 36 miles away from Anstruther. It was either ...at or something much further away. At least I could do a daily commute. The ...ost was a NATO position so I would be serving out my time working on the ...ATO Integrated Communications System (NICS) Telegraph Automatic Relay ...quipment. It was not radio work and neither was it a flying unit but it be for less ...an 3 years. The posting was accepted and I prepared to say my farewells to the ...ew that had never set a foot wrong in my almost 2 years with them.

...arewell "Architect" and so long to Phil Bayles, Nige Hocking, Bob Young, Dave ...eight, Katrina Balfour, Nikki Jones, Vinnie Sweeny, Jo Ham and the best Flight

Lieutenant I could have had as an Officer Commanding along with everybody else I have forgotten. Great times which will be missed.

Next and possibly the final stop: NATO Tare, Pitreavie Castle.

Chapter 6.
Royal Air Force Pitreavie Castle.
December 1991 – October 1994.
(All things must end).

My time in uniform was coming to an end and this would be my last posting unless I took up the option to sign on until I am an old man of 55. I must confess that after working at Kinloss I was tempted. We would give that option some serious consideration. Elaine was already settled in at home and had immediately found employment as Head Housekeeper at the Golf Hotel in Elie. The hotel was only a few miles along the coast from Anstruther with a good bus service. After sitting around for almost 2 years she was loving every minute of working again. Sam had settled in as well so everything at home was perfect. Elaine was more than content to stay put this time. If I did extend my career then I could end up anywhere which meant being away from home for long periods. To every positive there is always a negative so we would have to give that some thought as well. Anyway, for the foreseeable future I would be commuting to Pitreavie Castle.

Turning up for my arrival I was somewhat astonished by the fact that my new place of working was just a single concrete bunker on a hill surrounded by a security fence and a set of gates. These gates were unmanned and to gain access you had to use an intercom system. When you explained who you were the gates were opened and in you drove. At least they had a member of the RAF Police at the main entrance to check your identity before entering. The operations room consisted of one large computer system and little of anything else. This monster was known as the NICS TARE. In the same area was an office which housed two Flight Sergeants. After introducing myself I was given the necessary tour of the complex. I was totally confused by the fact that there were no aircraftmen/women in the building. It was explained that the manning for each of the 4 shifts was: 3 Sergeants and 1 Corporal. Instantly I concluded that this was a total waste of money. 3 SAC's and 1 Cpl would be a more effective manning level and a massive saving on the budget, but who am I to argue that point?. Apparently because it was a NATO facility that was the accepted manning levels for all the various stations using this communications system. The system consisted of the same set-up in all the nations of the North Atlantic Treaty Organisation form North America across to Turkey. The United

Kingdom had two such set-ups with the other one being at Northwood. That facility was the responsibility of the Royal Navy.

I knew at once that I was going to miss being in a "hands on" environment which was the system I had enjoyed so much at Kinloss and Fylingdales. This was just going to be babysitting a computer for 12 hours at a time. Not a lot to look forward to really. There were not even any supervisory duties for me to perform.

After the visit I was required to travel over the River Forth to RAF Turnhouse. This was the station that handled all the administration for the TARE site at Pitreavie Castle. It did not take me long to understand the military role for Turnhouse which was basically nothing at all. The only reason for this military base existing was to handle any Royal Flights that came into Edinburgh. The airport for Edinburgh was across the airfield from the Turnhouse entrance. When any members of the Royal family were arriving at the airport they could use the Turnhouse entrance which gave them some privacy. Arrival for me did not take long as this station was no bigger than Mount Batten. When I was in the Sergeant's Mess I was asked if I would be using the facility on a regular basis. I responded with "I live 50 miles away so the next time you see me is when I am clearing upon discharge". But for one visit in the next few years I was true to my word. With everything done I headed for home with a feeling of sadness in my heart. Was this the modern Royal Air Force at the end of the 20th Century had come to? If it was then I really did not want to be a part of it.

Before I got back to Anstruther my mind was already made up. This would be the last of my tours. Time to start looking to the future and getting my roots well established at home. I explained my thoughts to Elaine and her response was plain enough, "I will support you in whatever you decide". That was good enough for me. If I had wanted to remain in the Royal Air Force I would have been in with a chance of another promotion. While at Kinloss I had received two annual assessments which consisted of 7s & 8s with a recommendation of promotion. For me my last 3 assessments while at Pitreavie would now make no difference to my future so I was not going to do anything more than the minimum required.

A few days later I had to report for my first day shift and was introduced to my fellow watch workers, Richie Brown was as keen as mustard because he had just been promoted to Sergeant, Geoff Bayliss was our Corporal and sadly I just cannot remember the other Sergeant. I was positive that my new work mates would not mind me showing extraordinarily little interest in putting any effort to impress anybody with my intended minimum effort. The system that was in operation was totally different to all the ones I had worked on previously at oddington, Rudloe Manor and Hehn. For this reason my first few shifts consisted of sitting around, looking interested and keeping out of the way. Geoff had been in this post for some 5 years and knew everything about the system. Like myself he was on his last tour of duty but at least he managed to some interest. It was only a few weeks later that I was instructed to attend a training course at the NATO Communications and Information Systems School (NCISS), at Latina, Italy. The course of training was 4 weeks duration which seemed at the time somewhat excessive. Travel instructions and flight tickets were issued so in the middle of a very cold January 1992 I set off on a new adventure.

The first leg of the journey was a flight from Edinburgh to Heathrow and then board a British Airways flight to Leonardo da Vinci – Fiumicino airport, Rome. For some reason I was allocated "Club Class" seating on the Rome flight. Every other flight I had ever taken was either in the back of an RAF transport or with Caledonian Airways "cattle class". Even before the aircraft had left the runway I was being offered FREE alcoholic beverages by a stunning "trolley dolly". For the next 2 hours the drinks came along one after the other. By the time the aircraft landed and I got to passport control I was a little worse for wear. Following my written instructions to the letter I made it to the railway station and parted with thousands of Italian Lire for the train ticket to Latina. When arriving at the ticket office I had two bags with me, when I left I only picked one of them up. A stupid error on my part and I never even noticed until I was on the train heading south. This stupidity could be a problem as the bag that was left at the station contained among other things my joining instructions and £00 in Bank of Scotland notes. This money I could have exchanged for Lire at Heathrow but the rates on offer were a total rip-off. I never expected to see that piece of luggage again. The train was crawling along, the sun was out and it was warm in the carriage which instantly sent me to sleep. Waking up several hours later it was obvious that I had missed the stop for Latina and was somewhat lost in Central Italy. I jumped off at the next station where after a difficult conversation with the station master, he spoke no English and the only Italian I knew was "grazie" it became evident that there was no further service on that line heading North until early the next morning. The night sleeping on the platform was cold and uncomfortable but by the time the first train turned up I was perfectly sober. Things had not gone to plan but it was me that had caused the predicament by being greedy in "Club Class".

Finally I arrived at the Latina guardroom just before 10am on the Monday morning some 15 hours later than planned. Showing the required identity document I was given a printout of where everything on the base could be found. Luckily somebody with wisdom had produced an English arrivals package. The gentleman in this office then slid open a large window and handed me the holdall I had foolishly left at Rome station. In broken English he explained that it had been handed in at the station and when they checked the paperwork inside decided to send it on the next train for delivery to the air base. To my amazement nothing was missing and the envelope containing the cash was untouched. I was lucky that it had been handled by such an honest and decent person. Arriving at the accommodation block I dumped my bags and headed for the kitchen to sort out a hot drink. All of those who were joining me on the training course were already in there. They introduced themselves and seemed a decent enough group. Being a NATO course all who participated had to be fluent in English which made life easy for me being the only "Brit" on the course. As we chatted one of them asked why I was so much later than everybody else in arriving. Feeling a bit of an idiot I explained everything in detail. After that there were tears of laughter from 11 of the 12 in there. The one who was not doubled over was a guy from the Turkish Air Force. He had not understood a word of my story. His command of the English language was to say minimal at best. The ice had been broken and I knew that the next 4 weeks were going to be great fun.

I just had to enquire, why is everybody hanging around the accommodation block and not doing any actual training. It was explained that the training for the technicians and the operators was carried out at this location but there was only one computer system to play with. In the mornings the "techies" got to play with it and then in the afternoons we were let loose on it. Now spending the next 4 weeks doing half a day of work was not going to be very taxing, I was really impressed with this arrangement and decided that I would try to learn something. Lunchtime came and after eating together in the Italian mess we all headed off to our first session of learning. Guided to a classroom we were introduced to the "3 Amigos" who would be our instructors. Phil "Taff" Small (Royal Air Force), Chuck Fraley (US Air Force) and Gunther Ullrich (German Air Force). After that we all took turns at standing up front and officially introducing ourselves and giving a background to our service life. This was a mixed group of nationalities and some of us had led more eventful careers than the others. Again, the Turkish member had problems and the 3 amigos concluded he would not be in training for long. Next on the timetable was a question and answer paper for us to complete. All the questions were to do with military communications so most of us breezed through it in no time. Our Turkish friend was sat beside me looking totally perplexed so when I completed my paper I slid his over to me and filled in the questions with the correct answers. Luckily our instructing staff had left the room while this was going on. When we had completed this strenuous task our training day was already omplete. Off we all wandered in an orderly fashion to the mess for the evening meal.

Iaving no knowledge of Italian cuisine I decided to give the calamari a try with ome soggy pasta and a somewhat lumpy sauce. After 15 minutes of chewing he calamari was gently removed from my mouth and I just about managed to nish off the pasta. We all wandered back to our own kitchen and discussed the rst day together. The consensus was that the mess food was no way up to a ecent enough standard to put up with for a month. A bowl was placed on the ble and each of us put piles of lire into it. The Americans only had US dollars o they contributed the equivalent of about £50 each. This gave us a substantial ot to get our own supplies to live on. We already had everything in the kitchen. was fully equipped with fridge, freezer and micro-wave. The only thing iissing was a dish-washer. A rota was going to be needed to ensure the place id not end up looking like a disaster zone. All we needed to do was get some ipplies in from the town of Latina. That would not be a problem as we already ad plenty of transport.

efore I go further I need to introduce you to my fellow students.

rent Smith (Canada), Aniello Caiazza (Italy), Gerard Den Ouden Netherlands), Henning Pedersen (Norway), Lundy Hall (USA), Terry Williams JSA), Bart Gijbels (Belgium), Robert Wiley (USA), Frieda Achten Netherlands), Roland Hassforth (Germany) & Robert Leos (USA).

8 nations and not a "bad apple" among them. (Our instructors joined us for this course photo).

ransport was supplied by Roland who had driven from Germany, Bart who rove down from Belgium and Henning who had a hire car at his disposal. He ad been given everything you could ever want by the Norwegian government.

The car was hired for him because a private villa near Latina beach was put at his personal disposal. He never used this facility and decided to live with the rest of his course mates in the barrack accommodation. The defence ministry of Norway had not overlooked anything to make his stay extremely comfortable. As for our MoD, all I got was about £5 per day living overseas allowance.

It was decided that some of us would go into the town next morning to get in as many supplies we could carry and spend everything we had just collected. Suddenly 3 members of the technician's course decided they wanted to latch on to our group and added to the mountain of Lire and dollars. It was then off for showers and clean ups before we all went over to the NATO bar. This club was not available to Italian service members stationed on the base so it would not be overcrowded. As a duty-free establishment it meant much cheaper prices on the drinks. It was a nice club which would become our evening out for the rest of our time here. We had already decided to stick together for the duration and gathered enough seating around some tables to enjoy the evening. The rest of the course members insisted that as I was the "senior" in age only, I would be responsible for the budget. The Americans explained that just over 100 miles away there was a US Navy base in Naples. They could get access to the base and purchase anything we wanted from the shops on base. It was agreed that the 3 US Navy lads would be driven by Henning to the base the next morning and spend the dollars wisely. The rest of us would use the other 2 cars and sort out shopping from the local supermarkets. We had plenty of time to get this completed because we were not needed at the training school until after lunch.

Many beers and countless bottles of wine were consumed on our first evening. With the wine costing about £1.50 a litre it would have been rude to say no when asked if you wanted a drink. The other big seller at the bar was popcorn. Buckets of this salty delight were bought every night. It must have been a nightmare for the cleaning staff the next morning. It was close to midnight before we all fell out of the club and headed back to our single rooms for some shut-eye. Next day was going to be busy getting stocked up with the essentials for survival.

Nobody had any breakfast the next morning because none of us could face the Mess again and the cupboards in our kitchen were empty. Before we set of on our shopping expedition I made sure that the fridge and freezer were switched on as they would be needed. The US contingent had left incredibly early because it was a 4 hour round trip to Naples. Then four of us made our way to the supermarkets of Latina with bundles of Lira at our disposal. We found a large supermarket which had everything we needed. Like moths to a lantern, we males headed straight for the drink's aisles. Thankfully Frieda suggested it

ould be a good idea to buy some food first. She was so organised that she did
ne breakfast items followed by lunchtime snacks and finally essentials to knock
p a decent evening meal. As most of the course were Europeans one trolley
as stocked up with everything you needed for a Continental breakfast. For
1ose from the US & Canada trays of baked beans were added. With the solids
orted it was now the turn of the liquid supplies. Spirits were expensive but the
ost of any beer or wine was compared to the UK, unbelievably cheap. Local
ines were in 1 litre bottles and were cheaper than buying a bottle of water.
oon after our arrival back at the base the American contingent returned with
1eir supplies. Mountains of meat were sorted into the freezer. The T-bone
eaks were the size of a dinner plate and only cost $1 each. The facilities at
aples were heavily subsidised so everything was cheap. In their shopping was
omething called "refried beans" which I was to try that evening. It was
isgusting and I never bothered having that again.

oing in for training that afternoon our Turkish lad was called to one side by
ne of the office staff. That was the last we saw of him. It had come to the
tention of those in charge that, he had no command of the English language
1d would not be able to start, let alone complete the training. Obviously, Taff
1d the other instructors had noticed that somebody else had completed his test
aper on the previous day.

'e soon got into the routine of lounging in the mornings, learning in the
ternoons and partying in the club in the evening. Everything we needed for a
omfortable life was supplied in the accommodation block. There was a
levision room with a large television and video player. Previous courses had
onated a collection of videos and it soon became normal practice after the club
osed to settle down with a bottle of wine accompanied watching videos until
1e early hours. Along with our German (Roland) there were a couple of
erman Air Force techies in training as well. These lads had the same video
quest most nights. They loved watching "Blackadder goes forth". How they
1derstood the English humour I will never know.

NATO bar Latina with Roland & Bart.

With Frieda in the NATO bar.

We had three weekends to look forward to in Italy and were determined not waste that time hanging around the base drinking. Rome & Pompeii were musts for a visit. Roland however decided that it would be a good idea to drive to Rome one evening for a meal. It seemed a good idea as Latina to Rome was less than 60 miles. Seven of us decided to join him so he and Henning supplied the transport. Never in my life have I ever come across such awful driving standards. If you are of a nervous disposition I advise you never to drive anywhere near Rome, let alone inside the city itself. You must never use your indicators or use a roundabout correctly, to do so is a sign of weakness and other motorists will go all out to kill you. The one thing you must always use is the car horn, just leave your hand always resting on it. We found a nice restaurant and even though it was January the weather was warm enough to eat "al fresco". We were the only customers doing this which seemed strange until we noticed the stars being blocked out by flocks of starlings heading in to roost. Every tree in the avenue was covered with them and every vehicle was ombarded with guano. It was an enjoyable evening and on the return trip Henning became more adapt to the Italian style of driving.

The following Saturday was our day trip to Rome and for some reason a few of the from the Technicians course decided to join us. Jim, a Canadian stated that most of his course members were boring *****, hence some of them wanted to tag along with us. Not a problem as the 11 on the Operators course were getting on with no problems. There were to many of us to use the cars so we all piled down to the train station for the first train to Rome. Using the train meant that nobody had to stay on lemonade and chauffer us around. Frieda decided she wanted to see every historical tourist attraction in one day. I have no idea how many miles we covered but we visited everything from the Coliseum to the Vatican Gardens. A few even threw money into the Trevi fountain. I wonder if they have returned in the last 30 years.

With Frieda & Jimbo at the Coliseum.

With aching feet it was decided to find a bar and recover for a while. Being the gentleman that I am I offered to pay for the first round of drinks. Roland decided that he wanted to have a proper beer, it had to be "Lowenbrau". After half an hour wandering down alleys we found a bar that had this German lager on draught. We all squeezed in this tiny "pub" and I placed our order. When I got the bill for the first round I was amazed.

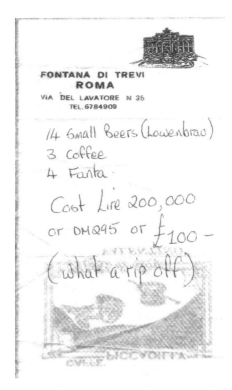

FONTANA DI TREVI
ROMA
ViA DEL LAVATORE N 35
TEL.6784909

14 Small Beers (Lowenbrau)
3 Coffee
4 Fanta.

Cost Lire 200,000
or DMQ95 or £100 -

(what a rip off)

If you ever travel to Rome make sure you take your refreshments with you.

Apart from the expense of the whole thing we had a great day out. What amazed me was just how may beggars with children were on the streets. You had to always keep a firm hand on your wallet. The number of historical building with graffiti all over them was a real eye-opener. The highlight for me even though I am an atheist was the Sistine Chapel. The artwork inside that building was stunning. It was also the day I discovered my dislike for heights. We went to the top of the chapel and peered over the balcony. Frieda peeled my hands of the safety barrier and I was then assisted back down to ground level. I was 37 years old and had never experienced such total panic in all my life. For some unknown reason even today I can fly with no problem but, put me on a ladder and I just freeze.

Monday was back to the learning routine and how we never got thrown of the course is still a mystery. Because we spent our mornings in the block kitchen having breakfast and drinking cheap wine we were somewhat worse for wear every time we arrived at the school. Obviously our instructors had grown use to such behaviour from the courses that had been before us. Gunther explained that we were no way as bad as some earlier courses. Taff found the whole thing amusing and Chuck just kept his opinions to himself. I will openly confess that

The worst offenders in our group were, yours truly along with the Norwegian and the Canadian.

Taff was of the same age as me and he had also done a "punishment tour" as an instructor at the Communications School in the UK. I got the impression that like me, he did not enjoy that experience. He invited me to his "hiring" in Latina for a curry one evening and it was a chance to meet his wife. It was a good evening and driving back in his Vauxhall Cavalier, which was a bit of a banger, he got immense pleasure at annoying Italian motorists. Because the continent of Europe drives on the wrong side of the road, headlight beams on British cars require deflectors. Taff could not be bothered with all that so even when driving on dipped beam it dazzled on-coming drivers. If flashed by them he would just give them full beam for an instant. He had heard about my travel problems arriving at Latina and too much amusement stated that if there had been a Wren on the course he would have picked us up from the airport. Sexist git that he was.

I still had an envelope full of cash from the Bank of Scotland to exchange and took it to the bank on the base. Handing it over the counter I asked for Lire in exchange. A £20 pound note was studied and then passed around all the bank staff. The manager enquired "what country are these from". I explained that they were British bank notes and gave him details of how Scotland had its own banks (3 of them) rather than use the notes issued by the Bank of England. It should be the same exchange rates, I explained. After much head scratching he said that he would have to contact head office to get an exchange rate. Could I come back tomorrow. Somewhat confused I agreed. Going back next day I got my piles of lira but at a 10% reduced exchange rate compared to any "Bank of England" notes. Apparently, bank notes from North of the English border were not recognised legal tender.

Our second weekend arrived and this time we would do a cultural trip to Pompeii. The three cars were loaded with enough food and drink to sustain us because going there "out of season" meant none of the tourist facilities would be open. Once again Frieda was insisting on seeing every inch of the place.

5000 lire for a little piece of history.

On our final weekend we all decided to start doing some serious studying on the course notes to save any possible embarrassment of failure. The final exams were only a few days away and still being united as a team we wanted everyone to be successful. The written element was no problem but for most of us when it came to the practical examination we were useless. On the Thursday we were tested in groups of three. Most of us had been enjoying the last of our supplies of beer and wine. If the instructors had not been there to guide us through we would never have even managed to switch the computer on. On behalf of our course, Thank you Taff Small, Chuck Fraley and Gunther Ullrich. With the course completed it was time to say our goodbyes and return to our respective countries.

14th Feb 1991. With Frieda and Smitty on the last day.

We had all achieved what we came to do and for the rest of the course it was another qualification with a chance of further promotion. Most of them would also find a little something extra in their pay packets from this day on. I do not know if this is true but the US Navy guys said they would be awarded yet another medal for completing the course.

14th Feb 1991. Bidding farewell to Smitty, Robert Wiley and Robert Leos.

Phil did the decent thing and next morning drove me to the airport in Rome. I thought at that time it would be the last time I would come across this humorous Welshman because I had less than 3 years to serve. Surprisingly even some 30 years later he is still one of my best friends. The daft sod even asked me to be "best man" when he married the lovely Jan on 28th April 2018.

Ticket in hand and perfectly sober I boarded the flight back to Heathrow for onward travel up to Edinburgh. However, on this flight I just drank coffee all the way. No way did I want to repeat the performance of my flight the other way a month earlier especially since I would have to drive home after getting to Edinburgh.

Flight ticket home in Club Class.

My time in Latina had been not just educational (yes I did learn something) but great fun with great people.

Once back in Anstruther I had a few days before going back to work as qualified and being able to play unsupervised on the computer. When back at work it became apparent that both the other Sergeants were as keen as mustard, and why not they had careers ahead of them. I would just leave them and Geoff get on with things, with me taking a backseat doing my best to keep out of any trouble. They all seemed content with the situation. In Anstruther I was getting well established in the local community so for me the rest of my career was just a job. I had begun counting the days until my "demob". On weekdays I did make some effort at doing some work because the day workers were around. However, on the night shifts and the weekends I did as little as possible. A weekend dayshift consisted of washing the car and watching The Simpsons in the rest room. For the next 18 months our system worked perfectly for me.

October 1993 rolled around in no time and I was now in my last year. Because I had served "the full term" I was entitled to as many resettlement courses, within a financial budget, as I desired. This was supposed to assist me in the transition to gaining employment in civilian life. I made sure I used every penny in the kitty and went on some totally useless training courses. One however that would be handy in the future was "garden wall construction". All these courses meant travel and accommodation all at the tax-payers expense. Being away for a least a week every month meant that I had been written off as effective staff at work. I was getting more than my fair share of stand-downs and turning up for a night shift was an exceedingly rare thing.

Somehow though my name came to the attention of the guardroom at RAF Turnhouse. I had never been called upon to carry out the duties of Orderly Sergeant since my arrival. They decided to rectify that point and I was given the odious task of sitting in the guardroom with four airmen controlling the entry to the base on a Sunday. Turning up I explained to the airmen that they could sort out who was doing what because all that was needed was one person controlling the main entrance at any time. I read the relevant Station Standing Orders (SSO) for my duty and signed as having read them. These included a clause which instructed us to keep the main gates open during daylight hours. This was purely for the benefit of the Edinburgh Flying Club. They used our entrance rather than the civilian airport entrance. Apparently, it then meant they did not have to cross the runway to get to their clubhouse. The first of the guards proceeded out to do his first hour on duty. With the rain lashing down he got drenched and immediately his morale hit rock bottom. I then decided to use a little common sense and told them to close the gates and observe any arrivals from the guardroom. This solved the problem of them continually getting soaked and meant only a minor disruption to anybody wanting access. My only movement outside the guardroom for the next 24 hours was a visit to the Sergeant's Mess for something to eat. Once we were relieved of our duties the lads went on their way and I headed home to get some sleep.

I had been home for less than 30 minutes when somebody from the police flight at Turnhouse phoned me. He said I had to report to OC Police Flight at once. I told him I was at home, had not slept so it would have to wait. "If you do not come in now, we will come and get you" was his response. About an hour later I was back at Turnhouse being interviewed by 2 "over the top" RAF Policemen. They even had a recorder going to take down the interview. This was all over the fact that I had left the gates shut while doing the guard duty. The pair of them were so gung-ho I just looked at them and said "Jeez, the way you two are acting, anybody would think I had been passing stuff to the Russians". Interview over I got home again and finally managed to get to bed. As soon as I got to work for the next day shift I was taken into the office and issued with (yet another) F252 charge sheet. OC Police was charging me with "Failure to comply with Station Standing Orders". The Station Commander of RAF Turnhouse would be hearing the charge later that morning. As I drove over the Forth road bridge to Turnhouse I just thought to myself: You just could not make this sort of farce up. I was asked why I did not open the gates I just responded with "I used my initiative and common sense, why have somebody stood for an hour in pouring rain, for no sensible reason". Eventually, I was given a reprimand for my actions. As I left I walked up to OC Police and whispered, "You are a first degree knob". There was nothing he could do about my comment as nobody else had heard it. This whole sorry farce only came to the attention of the police flight because one of my fellow communicators from Pitreavie was mouthing off at breakfast in the Mess about the gates being shut.

was only a few weeks after my charge that the Chief Clerk from the general ffice phoned me and asked if I wanted to extend my service until age 55. You n imagine what my response to that was.

ime was now drifting by so I started sending in job applications for civilian nployment. I covered the whole of East Fife because there was absolutely thing on offer in Anstruther. When I started my terminal leave, an extra 30 ys on top of the normal annual leave, I had not received a single response to ny of my applications. It looked like I would be queueing at the job centre very on. My final trip to Pitreavie and Turnhouse was to clear for a final clearance. anding in my identity card was like parting with a good friend. When I drove vay from that military establishment I had mixed emotions. I was going to ally miss "the good old days" but at the same time glad to be leaving the odern Royal Air Force. A lot had changed since turning up at Swinderby on a ld October morning in 1972.

or my time at NICS Tare Pitreavie Castle I must thank; Bryn Roberts, Geoff ayliss & Richie Brown for their friendship and patience. It was not all bad and y four weeks in Latina had been an experience I will never forget.

y first operational posting in 1973 had been to RAF Lyneham. My time there ill holds so many happy memories. I returned in 2017 after arranging a visit r myself and the "Lyneham Lovelies". Gaining access to the old terminal ilding we made our way to what was the Communications Centre. It was once bustling hive of activity but now the sight that greeted us brought tears to my es.

The remains of my first operational posting, Communications Centre Royal Air Force Lyneham (1973). These pictures were taken on a visit in 2017 prior to the demolition of the Air Terminal building. An incredibly sad experience. Lyneham is no longer an operational air base. It was closed in 2012. The complete

complex was handed over to the British Army and is now the home of the Defence School of Electronic and Mechanical Engineering.

t had been a pleasure to serve Her Majesty Queen Elizabeth II for 22 years. Vhen asked if I would join the Royal Air Force today, I always give the same nswer: "Only if it was with the same people and we could time-travel back to 972".

And finally.

October 1994 – Who knows when?.

(A shock to the system).

faving had no success in seeking employment I began losing all self-respect for 1yself. Over the next year my consumption of alcohol, mostly whisky, reached level which any sensible person would class as unacceptable. Along with this I ecame subject to massive bouts of depression. Naturally life at home was ecoming more stressful for Elaine. She tolerated my mood swings and ehaviour for just over a year. Finally unable to take any more she moved out of 1e family home. We agreed that even though she had done everything possible) hold our marriage together, it was finally over.

spent the next 4 years drifting from place to place and from living rough to 1ding up in a stunning bachelor pad overlooking the Port of Ramsgate. I :tempted various positions of employment but walked away from them all. A :w relationships with younger & older ladies were also attempted but all led to ailure, purely because not one of them was Elaine.

ll of that is a story for another day.

7hen I left the world of communications in the military I was cursing the lvancements in technology. Today, my attitude has changed drastically. If it 1d not been for the Internet I would not be in contact with hundreds of my iends, some of whom I still class as family more than friends.

fy last words go to Dafydd Manton for talking me into putting my story into int. **"Thank you, Cold War Penguin".**

Printed in Great Britain
by Amazon

71569111R00048